The House that Jack Built

A Memoir

We Really Do become what we think about!

Jack Winter

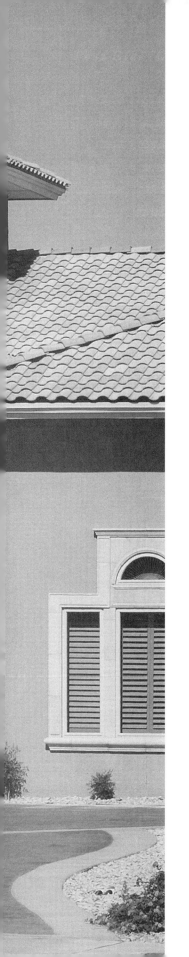

The House that Jack Built

A Memoir

Jack Winton

The House that Jack Built, A Memoir by Jack Winton. Copyright © 2013 by Jack Winton

Printed in the United States of America. All rights reserved.
No part of this book may be used or reproduced in any manner whatsoever without written permission, except in case of brief quotations for reviews. For information write Winton & Associates, Inc., 6300 Escondido Drive, El Paso, Texas, 79912, or call 915-584-8629.

FIRST EDITION
10   9   8   7   6   5   4   3   2   1

Publisher's Cataloging-in-Publication Data

Winton, Jack, 1933-
    The house that Jack built, a memoir / written by Jack Winton — 1st edition. — El Paso, TX : Winton & Associates, Inc., 2013.
    320 p. : ill., maps ; 26 cm.
    ISBN 978-0-615-73733-1
    1. Winton, Jack, 1933-.   2. El Paso (Tex.)—Biography.   3. Character.   4. Success—Psychological aspects.   5. Life skills.   6. Business.   7. Sales and Marketing.   I. Title.

Book and jacket design by
Vicki Trego Hill of El Paso, Texas.

Cover photographs of Winton home by Bill Faulkner.

Edited by Ellen Claire Shaeffer, Dr. Richard Teschner,
and Elena Marinaccio.

Printed on acid free paper
∞

*This book is dedicated to my family,
beginning from those I met in my earliest memories,
through those who are yet to be born.
At this point I have six children,
ten grandchildren and four great-grandchildren.
To them and their offspring,
I give this story of my life.*

Contents

Acknowledgements *xi*
Poem: "This is the House that Jack Built" *xii*
Introduction *xv*

Part I. A Sense of Humor

1. Traded for a Cow 3
2. Life in the Country 9
3. That Old-Time Religion 16
4. The Best Milkshake in Stigler 20
5. The Great White Hunter 29

Part II. Creativity

6. Picking Weeds in Clovis, New Mexico 35
7. Stage Struck 39
8. Not So Easy Reading 44
9. Wedding Bells 50
10. In the Army 56
11. Good People 61

Part III. Fortitude

12. Family Style 67
13. What Size, Ma'am? 71
14. Making Bacon 76
15. High Flying 83

Part IV. Curiosity

16. What's Real Estate? 91
17. Selling Property Door-to-Door 97
18. Can't Say No 106
19. Building the Business 110
20. Meeting the Master 115
21. RTPSF/RWF 121

Part V. Loyalty

22. Marty, Jack and Jack 129
23. Country Club Living 136
24. My Life in a Cardboard Box 140
25. Joy 147
26. Green Fingers 159
27. The Newlyweds 166

Part VI. Fairness

28. Down by the Rio Grande 175
29. New Partners 179
30. Santa Teresa 183
31. The Deal Falls Apart 188
32. Up in the Air 192

Part VII. Humility

33. Blowin' and Goin' 201
34. Train Wreck 205
35. Back in the Saddle 211

36. God, Please Give Me Another Boom
(and I Promise Not to Blow it)   217

37. Accent on Success   229

Part VIII. Integrity

38. The First Key to Success: Our Product   237
39. The Second Key to Success: Our People   246
40. The Most Important Key to Success: Our Customers   258
41. Non-Stop Learning   262
42. Looking Back and Looking Forward   273

Notable People in My Life Not Mentioned Earlier

In Stigler, Oklahoma   285
In Clovis, New Mexico   285
From the Army Days   287
From the Eastern New Mexico University Days   288
From the Meat Packing Days   289
From the Early Real Estate and Homebuilding Days   290
People from El Paso   291
Public Figures Whose Philosophies Helped Me   295

Appendices

A. Poems to Live (and Laugh) By   296
B. Books that Have Made Me a Success   300
C. Ten Things to Look for When Buying a New Home   301

Acknowledgements

I want to thank Dusty Henson of the El Paso Saddleblanket Company for convincing me that I should write this book. He told me it would be easy and fun. He was partially right, but he put me in touch with Bill Crawford, who I also owe a thanks to for helping us put the book together, for giving it structure, for having the vision of what the final product should be, and for keeping us within certain literary boundaries. I am grateful that Ellen Claire Shaeffer and her experience at writing biographies added a touch I could not have gotten from anyone but her. Dr. Richard Teschner brought his considerable knowledge of linguistics and his skill at editing that I am thankful for. And, many thanks to Elena Marinaccio for the final copy edit. Vicki Trego Hill is a masterful designer and the final look and feel of the book would not have been possible without her. I thank Lunell Winton for providing old photographs and the Milburn Moore family for the video. I thank Nhi Hong and Verbal Ink for their excellent transcription service, my daughter Monica for her sharp eye on the final proof, and also I thank my son Scott for his help in making this book become a reality. It would probably have been completed a lot sooner without his participation, but not nearly as good. Lastly, I thank my wife and life partner Joy. She read every draft and laughed at the jokes every time she read them. She added things and took things out so that the final product is just a glimpse of the beautiful life we have had together.

This is the House that Jack Built

This is the house that Jack built.
This is the malt that lay in the house that Jack built.

This is the rat that ate the malt
That lay in the house that Jack built.

This is the cat that killed the rat
That ate the malt that lay in the house that Jack built.

This is the dog that worried the cat
That killed the rat that ate the malt
That lay in the house that Jack built.

This is the cow with the crumpled horn
That tossed the dog that worried the cat
That killed the rat that ate the malt
That lay in the house that Jack built.

This is the maiden all forlorn
That milked the cow with the crumpled horn
That tossed the dog that worried the cat
That killed the rat that ate the malt
That lay in the house that Jack built.

This is the man all tattered and torn
That kissed the maiden all forlorn
That milked the cow with the crumpled horn
That tossed the dog that worried the cat
That killed the rat that ate the malt
That lay in the house that Jack built.

This is the priest all shaven and shorn
That married the man all tattered and torn
That kissed the maiden all forlorn
That milked the cow with the crumpled horn
That tossed the dog that worried the cat

That killed the rat that ate the malt
That lay in the house that Jack built.

This is the cock that crowed in the morn
That woke the priest all shaven and shorn
That married the man all tattered and torn
That kissed the maiden all forlorn
That milked the cow with the crumpled horn
That tossed the dog that worried the cat
That killed the rat that ate the malt
That lay in the house that Jack built.

This is the farmer sowing his corn
That kept the cock that crowed in the morn
That woke the priest all shaven and shorn
That married the man all tattered and torn
That kissed the maiden all forlorn
That milked the cow with the crumpled horn
That tossed the dog that worried the cat
That killed the rat that ate the malt
That lay in the house that Jack built.

This is the horse and the hound and the horn
That belonged to the farmer sowing his corn
That kept the cock that crowed in the morn
That woke the priest all shaven and shorn
That married the man all tattered and torn
That kissed the maiden all forlorn
That milked the cow with the crumpled horn
That tossed the dog that worried the cat
That killed the rat that ate the malt
That lay in the house that Jack built.

—A POPULAR BRITISH NURSERY RHYME AND CUMULATIVE TALE
ORIGINALLY PUBLISHED IN 1755.

Introduction

I GUESS YOU COULD SAY that I'm a pretty lucky fellow. Okay, I also worked pretty hard. Growing up on a farm in Oklahoma, I learned how to work, and I eventually built a multi-million dollar business.

A few years ago, I decided that I wanted to write the important details of my life. It's for my family and my customers so that they can know who I am and what I do.

I hope my story will inspire you, and I hope you will have some fun along the way. There are actually some valuable lessons I share.

Some might say that, "Other than his bankruptcy, his story sounds like a bed of roses." That might be true, but I think it reflects the basic core of my personality. I am a positive person! I do not like negativity, nor do I let it be a part of me. I have tried to live this way ever since I learned that it is my attitude that the world responds to. If I am negative, I get negativity back. So, a long time ago I made a determined commitment to be positive. You will see that throughout the book. Earl Nightingale, a radio broadcaster who spent his life looking for, and then communicating, the secrets of success says we become what we think about. He also says that when we have the right attitude and the right expectations, the universe will respond with the right things when we need them. This has happened to me all my life: people, things, opportunities all came at a time when I needed them. They still do. I hope that this book, the story of my life, is a testament to the fact that the

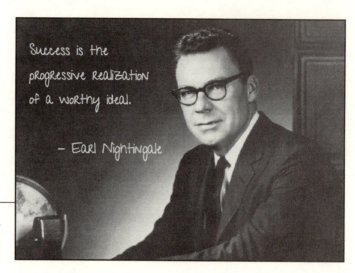

Earl Nightingale

universe gives us exactly what we ask of it. I hope those who read this book can take that fundamental universal law and consciously make whatever life they desire to benefit themselves and others. This is what I share with you, to all who read this book, these are some of the things I learned along the way.

You will also see throughout the book that I tell a lot of jokes. That's me. I love humor and I love making people laugh. I have found that sharing a laugh with someone, especially a stranger, is one of the best ways to break the ice. It creates common ground between people and makes us feel good. When we can feel good together, then we will likely be friends and we will probably do business together.

I would sometimes begin my speaking engagements by saying to my audience, "My job here today is to speak. Your job is to listen. If you get finished before I do, then please hold up your hand." But in this instance, my job is to write, and yours is to read. If you decide you are finished before I am, please lead me to believe that you did read the entire book when you next see me.

Also, I was taught that if you cannot say something good about someone, don't say anything at all. So if you know me and don't find your name in the book, please don't think this might be a reason why you aren't mentioned.

PART I
A Sense of Humor

"The deepest craving of most young people is to be liked by their fellow students. They want to be accepted and looked up to by the other students. They begin to do what the other kids are doing, and the other kids begin to do what they are doing, and everyone acts just like everyone else. They dress alike; they talk alike; they laugh at the same things—even when it isn't funny."

—EARL NIGHTINGALE

One

Traded for a Cow

My story starts on the day I was born, September 20, 1933. I was born to Thomas Elmer Winton and Opal Louise King Winton. It was the depths of the depression. Nobody had any money. There just wasn't any around. We lived way out in the Oklahoma countryside in a little settlement in Haskell County called Beaver Mountain, so my Mom gave birth to me at home.

When she went into labor, my dad got the doctor to come from Quinton, Oklahoma,—ten miles away—to help with my delivery. Dad told him, "I don't have any money to pay you but I'll give you a cow." So the doctor took the cow. My dad jokingly used to say he thought the doctor got cheated.

My father's family, I believe, came from somewhere in Kentucky, and they settled in Quinton. His father's name was Thomas. They called him Tom. I don't remember him at all, but my older sisters do. Apparently he was a very kindly, gentle man, and the children gravitated to him and loved him. He had a team of very spirited mules. One day when he was harnessing them in the lot of the barn at the house in Quinton, something scared one of the mules and Tom jumped.

A rope got wrapped around my grandfather's leg and that scared the animals worse. They ran all around the lot dragging him, and he couldn't get loose. It was an area with a lot of rocks and it killed him, just like that, one Sunday afternoon.

My grandmother remained single for a long time until she married someone called Lee Nations. We never really got to know him.

My father's name was Thomas Elmer Winton, but he mostly went by T. E. He signed everything T. E. Winton.

He left home when he was sixteen. I guess like a lot of teenagers, he did not see eye to eye with his parents. He bummed his way west on the railroad, even crawling and riding underneath the cars, riding the rods as they called it, until he got to California. Then he lied about his age and joined the U.S. Navy. He spent four years in the Navy and got tattooed like the kids do today. He got out of the Navy with no education, never even graduated from high school. When he got out he fell madly in love with this beautiful gal, my mother, who was an Indian (or a Native American, to be politically correct). He finally convinced her to marry him.

My mother's father was a Choctaw named Charlie King. My mother's mother died in childbirth when my mother, Opal, was two years old. Her father suffered from depression after losing his wife and child and in his depression, he left. Nobody saw him or heard from him for ten years.

So Opal's maternal grandfather, Garibaldi Farrill, took her and raised her as if she was one of his children. My mother grew up with his daughters who were much older, but they were always like sisters to my mother. That was in eastern Oklahoma, in the vicinity of Stigler, forty-six miles west of Fort Smith, Arkansas.

When my mother was three years old, her grandfather took her to the necessary authorities and registered her birth as a member of the Choctaw tribe. She was given eighty acres of land in Oklahoma and after she married, we farmed that land, which we called "the place

The earliest picture I have of my mother, Opal Louise King Winton. She was in her early thirties when this photo was taken.

over on the bluff." It was very near Beaver Mountain.

We all called Grandfather Garibaldi "Pa" and when he was about sixty-five he came to live with our family and stayed with us until he passed away. He was a great help to my mother. She had seven children: my oldest sister was Polly, my next sister was Louise, I had a brother Thomas who didn't survive childhood, and a sister named Bette. I was next, and then a brother named Don Ray who also didn't survive childhood, and then a sister named Becky. So it was me and four sisters. With five children under one roof, we really appreciated Pa's help. He was the babysitter for all of us.

I remember how Pa taught me to play checkers. When I was about three, I would sit on a nail keg and he would sit on a chair opposite me. He made a checkerboard by taking a square piece of wood, drawing a grid on it, and darkening every other square. We used soda pop bottle caps for the pieces. And I got to be a pretty good checker player by the time I was five or six years old.

> *You know there is a joke about playing checkers. There was a knock on the door and an old man says, "Come on in." This guy walks in, and the old man is sitting at a checkerboard and across from him is a Collie dog, and this guy says, "What are you doing, what's going on?"*
>
> *And the old man says, "We're playing checkers, we'll be through in just a minute."*
>
> *And this guy says, "Are you kidding me? You mean that dog knows how to play checkers?"*
>
> *And the old man says, "Well, yeah."*
>
> *"This has got to be the smartest dog I've ever seen."*
>
> *And the old man says, "He ain't so smart, I beat him over half the time."*

Actually, I've run across a checker player or two in my time. I always say, "Hey, I'll take you on." And I get beat pretty regularly.

My mom and dad, Thomas Elmer (T. E.) and Opal Winton.

My dad worked at a zinc smelter in Henryetta, Oklahoma, from the time I can remember until the mid-1940s. He farmed as well. He worked on our little farm, leased land and farmed that too. In Henryetta, he and another fellow shared a very sparse apartment. They would travel to Henryetta, work double shifts, finish a week's work in three days, go back home and do farming. My dad usually farmed four or five parcels of land of his own. He just couldn't seem to get enough to satisfy his ambitions.

As if he didn't have enough to do, my dad turned the living room of our house into a neighborhood grocery store. I used to go with him to the wholesale house in Okmulgee, Oklahoma, to pick up the goods. We'd load up the pickup with cases of goods, drive them back to Beaver Mountain, unpack the goods and stock the shelves. Our house was *the* country store in Beaver Mountain.

My mom ran the grocery store and my dad ran the farms. About the time I got big enough to stay on a horse, I became his messenger. He would say, "You saddle up Old Blossom and ride over there to the bluff and tell Mac Spears that I want him to do this and this and that," and bingo, I'd take off. I practically lived on Old Blossom for years and loved every minute of it.

My dad worked as much as he could, but he did hire some workers. Mac Spears was one fellow who worked for my dad for many years. One day, Mac had an appendicitis attack. We put him in the car and headed for the doctor in Quinton. Old Mac was hurting so bad, he asked us if he could get out of the car and run. Unfortunately, poor Old Mac did not survive. Life in the country was tough.

My mom and my dad were married for a total of forty-five years and raised seven children. My dad didn't drink, but he smoked a lot. The smoking and his work in the zinc smelter both contributed to the emphysema that killed him in 1968. My mother was born October 25, 1905 and lived until 1998. She had a long run of it and always had her memory.

My dad and my mom worked hard their whole lives. They instilled in me a work ethic that has served me well. It's something I am truly grateful for, and for the lessons I learned growing up in rural Oklahoma.

"We are now, and will become, what we think about."
—Earl Nightingale

Two

Life in the Country

As I mentioned, we lived way out in the country on a farm in the settlement of Beaver Mountain, Oklahoma. We had no electricity, no indoor plumbing; the toilet was about fifty yards behind the house. It was what we called the outhouse. I don't think most Americans today can comprehend what it felt like to have to walk to the outhouse on a cold winter night.

> *There was one cold winter night in December with snow and ice, and the rancher had to go to the bathroom. He knew how cold it was and how far it was to the outhouse so he put on his overalls, and his mackinaw and his overshoes and his hat and lit a lantern and made his way through the snow to the outhouse.*
>
> *When he opened the door, he held the lantern up and inside he saw a little old man dressed in red with a long white beard who was standing up there on the seat with his hand down in the hole.*

Suddenly the old man pulled up a little reindeer by the horns and wiped its face a little bit and slapped it and said, "Dadgum you Blitzen, I told you the Schmidt house."

Members of my family tell a lot of stories about when I was growing up. When I was about two years old I dropped a can of lye on my big toe. I've had an uneven toenail on the big toe of my left foot ever since.

During the days of the WPA (Works Progress Administration, a Depression-era public works program), there were a lot of black folks living in our community (or African Americans to be politically correct), and they would shop at our store. When they got their paycheck they would come and pay their bill, and my folks always gave them a candy bar. Well, there was this huge guy named Charlie Loveless. I will never forget him. Inevitably he would sit on the porch to eat his candy bar and he would call me over. I would sit on his lap and we would alternate bites of his candy bar. He'd take a bite and then give me a bite. Nothing tasted quite as good.

When I was still young, we moved many miles away to a little farming community named Salem, Oklahoma. It wasn't an incorporated town or anything, just an area near Henryetta. We lived there for a year or two. It had a one-room schoolhouse, and I rode a school bus to school. I remember attending second grade, but I didn't really learn very much.

What I enjoyed most was fishing in the pond down behind the house. I'd catch a little ol' fish, a perch, and bring it home. I'd try to talk my mom into cooking one for me, but I don't think she ever did.

My dad gave me a single shot .22 rifle when I was about seven and I really did get good with it. I used to take it down with me to fish, and I'd set up my little hook with the cork on it so if it moved, I knew I had a fish. While I was waiting for that to happen, I'd sit around with my .22 and if a little lizard would crawl up on a rock, I'd shoot it. I used to hit them square in the middle almost every time.

Right across the road from our house was an Indian campground where they had these little huts. It was deserted most of the time so we'd play around there, but then one time all the Indians converged for a big pow-wow, so I spent quite a bit of time observing those folks. I'd sneak around and hide behind the trees and watch them. It was quite a big party.

My father farmed with a team of mules, but he always had lots of horses. He had an old mare, and I mean an old mare, named Babe. Ol' Babe was very gentle and probably couldn't even run. My dad taught me to ride her when I was four or five years old. I'd follow Dad around. He would go do his farming work and I'd come trudging along on Ol' Babe. I was on that horse all day.

I ran the mules a little, but I was not really big enough to handle them. I recognized what needed to be done, but for me to do it was another matter. We grew peanuts, corn, cotton—lots of cotton. We chopped cotton walking up and down the rows, chopping the weeds and thinning out the cotton plants so that they would have room to grow, and then we'd pick cotton in the fall. Schools even let out for a three- or four-week period so all the school children could help harvest.

There was one guy who worked every year for us chopping cotton named Glen Tucker. He always used to sing,
"There'll be joy on that day
When we hear Tom Winton say,
We are through choppin' cotton for the year…"

We didn't have much money, but we still managed to celebrate holidays and birthdays.

> *As far as Christmas stories go, it has been established without question that women have been ragging on their husbands forever. The Bible even states that Mary rode Joseph's ass all the way into Bethlehem.*

This is the two-room schoolhouse I attended on Beaver Mountain. I served as the janitor for a period of time.

Beaver Mountain had a two-room schoolhouse, grades one through six in one room with a teacher, and grades six through twelve in the other room with a teacher. They usually made a deal with one of the students to work as the janitor. When I was in the fourth or fifth grade and lived about a half mile from the school, they gave me that job. And it was a pretty good job to have.

At the end of the day when everybody left I would take all the erasers out on the storm cellar roof, which was concrete, and beat all the chalk dust out of them. Then I would wash all the blackboards, put down floor sweep, a dust collector, all over the floor and sweep the two rooms until they were clean.

In the winter time I would go out to the coal house, which was a hundred feet away, and bring in buckets full of coal for the stove. I gathered some pine knots from the schoolyard which also served as fuel. I'd get up at five in the morning in the freezing cold weather and build a fire in each of the rooms and stay long enough to see that they were going well, then go back home, have breakfast, help with milking the cows, and then come back to school at nine o'clock. That job paid five dollars a month.

That five dollars a month was a lot of money. Pa, my great-grandfather, gave me a little leather pouch to keep my money in. When I got paid I would find a way to get that check cashed ASAP. I'd put all that money in the little leather pouch and hide it. From time to time though, I'd get it out, pull the money out, count it, look at it, feel it, and put it back and save it. That money was important to me. I guess because it was so hard to come by. Money was scarce in those days.

A neighbor owned a big brood sow that birthed a bunch of piglets. When they were weaned, he wanted to sell them, so I went over and bought two piglets from him. In fact, he put them in a gunny sack. They were little bitty things, didn't weight more than four or five pounds apiece. I brought them home carrying them in the toe sack.

I bought a hundred-pound bag of shorts (called "mill run shorts") for twenty-five cents. It was very rich stuff that sort of fell away in the process of milling feed. We took our milk and ran it through a separator, where the skim milk comes out of a big spout and the cream comes out of a little spout. You'd turn the crank to separate the cream, and we just threw away the skim milk, which is the 2% milk we pay so much for today. I would very carefully mix my mill run shorts with the skim milk to make a nice thick pudding, and feed that to my pigs. I practically spoon fed them and boy did they do well. They would follow me everywhere and my mother used to get very upset because they'd follow me into the house and if I didn't close the door very fast, they'd get right in behind me.

We slaughtered hogs every year and smoked the bacon. We had a smokehouse and at breakfast every morning we'd lay a slab of bacon down and slice off thin pieces to fry. When we got through there'd be a meat skin about thirty inches long and twelve or thirteen inches wide that we'd normally throw away. But I would save them and grease my little pigs with them. I'd rub their hides.

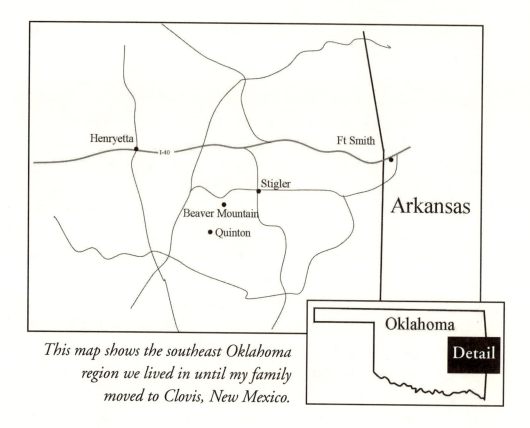

This map shows the southeast Oklahoma region we lived in until my family moved to Clovis, New Mexico.

There was a pig buyer named Cecil Argo who came through the countryside about once a month with a pickup and he'd buy people's hogs. Of course he knew the market value and, of course, the farmers didn't. When my pigs got up to about 150 or 160 pounds he kept stopping by to see if I would sell them, but I was reluctant to part with them. So I kept feeding them and shining them and he kept raising the price. I paid ten dollars for both of those pigs, and I put in a couple of hundred-pound bags of food. He paid me about $130 for them. I felt like a millionaire.

My grandmother was one of the few people with whom I shared the secret of my wealth, from cleaning the school and then investing in the pigs and then selling them. I remember when I was a little boy, maybe seven or eight, and she put me on her lap and looked me right in the eye and said, "You are going to be a very wealthy businessman someday."

I thought about that off and on for so many years.

I invested that hundred dollars in a horse, Danny. Danny Boy and I were the best of friends. He and the other horses would roam around in a fairly large pasture, about forty acres right behind the house. I'd step out there and could see the horses, and I would yell, "Danny" and he'd raise his head up and look around, and come running at me just as fast as he could.

The big mistake I ultimately made was selling him to somebody and investing that money in a Cushman motor scooter. It ended my investing in things that would make me money and started my investment in something which cost money—gas, oil, tires and all the things that go with owning a motorized vehicle. But my grandmother's words kept coming back to me through the years and I began to really believe them.

Napoleon Hill, in Think and Grow Rich, *said "Whatever the mind of man can conceive and believe, it can achieve."*

Three

That Old-Time Religion

IN RURAL OKLAHOMA, there was no question about it: everyone went to church. We went to the Baptist church. The church was about a block from the school in Beaver Mountain and it was called Mountain Home Baptist Church. We went all the time. We'd go every night when a visiting minister would come through the area with a revival.

> *A cowboy saddled his horse one Sunday morning and rode through the snow and the cold to church. When he arrived, nobody else was there except him and the preacher. The preacher saw him come in and proceeded to preach a two-hour sermon. When he finished he stood at the entry door, shook the cowboy's hand as he was leaving and asked: "How did you like the sermon?" The cowboy looked at the preacher and said: "You know, Reverend, when I go out on a cold snowing morning to feed my herd, and only one straggly steer shows up, I don't dump the whole damn load on 'em."*

I was baptized in the Baptist church when I was twelve. They did baptisms in the creek that ran through Beaver Mountain, in the round hole where the water was deeper. The preacher walked out in the water in his robe. And he put his hand out and covered my nose and held my mouth and said his words and put me under water. I'm in good shape, since it was a full dunking. My boys were raised Methodist, so they only got a sprinkling.

> *This man died and went to heaven. St. Peter was giving him a tour and pointed over in a direction and said, "Whatever you do here, please be sure and not go to that part of heaven. If you do find yourself over there, tiptoe away real quietly so that no one sees you or hears you."*
>
> *The man asked, "What's going on in that part of heaven?"*
>
> *St. Peter says, "The religious people are over there and they think they are the only ones here."*

My sister Bette was much more religious than I was. She and I were very close. She was just about two years older than me and served as my guardian angel. She wasn't afraid of anything. She wasn't afraid of the boogie man himself.

Walking from the school to our home, a half mile or so, every day during those early years, we'd run into a red-headed boy, kind of a big old gawky kid, named Weathers. He did everything he possibly could to harass me. When we were walking home on the dirt road with a ditch on either side, he'd walk over and ease me into the bar ditch. He did this two or three times. I'd get back up on the road and keep walking, and he'd catch up.

Finally Bette told him, "Don't do that anymore." Sure enough, he did it again and to his complete surprise and amazement, she whopped him right in the middle of his face with her fist and just beat the crap out of him. He never bothered me again.

Besides church, there wasn't much entertainment on Beaver Mountain. My elder sisters and my mother liked to listen to soap operas on the radio. They loved them and they did not want to be interrupted, so they would send me out. "Go out," they told me, "Go find something to do."

I knew that there was a radio antenna that ran pretty high on the house to a pole. I don't know where I got the idea but I knew that if you put a piece of metal against the antenna, it would interrupt the transmission. So I spent hours up on the roof, holding metal against the antenna listening to them down below: "Wonder what's going on with the radio?"

We ate homegrown vegetables from the garden. A skinny kid, I really never had much appetite. I was six feet one-and-a-half inches tall and only weighed 133 pounds when I went into the Army at age nineteen. Bette had a much bigger appetite, and ate all the leftovers, but she never gained an extra pound.

Even today, I have an appreciation for the value of food and hate to see food wasted. I still can't help comparing relative value of food on a menu. I look at something for twenty-seven dollars and I find something for twelve dollars of similar food value, so why don't I just eat that? I don't think there's any circumstance that would require me to be so frugal for the rest of my lifetime, but still these habits are there.

> *Why don't Baptists make love standing up?*
> *Someone might see them and think they are dancing.*

I can quote lots of Bible scriptures. After I learned to read, my sister Bette and I would read the Bible every night by kerosene lamplight. We would sit down and take turns reading a verse until we completed a chapter, and then we'd start at the beginning and go all the way through, Genesis to Revelations. Two of my favorites were John 3:16 and the Twenty-third Psalm.

The Bible is a good book. It's got a lot of good material in it.

There's a story about this guy who had a date with this beautiful young lady and he had never taken her out before and while she was finishing getting ready he saw the Bible on her coffee table. Trying to impress her, when she came out of the bedroom ready to go, he said, "Oh, I see you have some of Holly Bibble's work."

Mom was more religious than Dad, but Dad tolerated it. Later in his life, the church they were attending in Quinton needed to construct a new building. The congregation was trying to raise the money for the church, to build the spire, and my father said, "I will take care of that. Build it and send me the bill." By the time he passed away he was completely religious.

Everything you have came to you as a result of using your mind. This includes your work, your relationships, your philosophy of life, your religion, your possessions, everything. Experts say that we use probably less than ten percent of our mental capacity. Imagine what we could do if we could increase that.

Four

The Best Milkshake in Stigler

When I was twelve or thirteen, my family moved into the city of Stigler. The reason we moved was that my father ran into financial difficulties. One year, he planted twenty acres of peanuts and they sold at a high price. The next year he leased land from everybody he could and planted two hundred acres of peanuts. It just so happens that everybody in the country did the same thing. He harvested the peanuts and stored them in an empty house. While they were still curing, we'd go build fires in the fireplace and keep it burning all night, but those peanuts just rotted. My dad couldn't sell any peanuts, and he lost everything. Mentally, he never really did recover from that venture.

For the first time, we were living in a city. Our house was nice. We originally lived in a house called a shotgun house: you could shoot a shotgun in the front room and the shot would pass through the whole house without hitting anything. The house in Stigler had a living room (we called it a front room), a dining room, a kitchen and a door out the back. Over on the right side of the house were three bedrooms. There was a screened-in back porch where I stayed; that was my room. It was cold sometimes.

> *"We never really grow up.
> We only learn how to act in public."*
>
> —Bryon White

Since he had a little bit of experience in the store business from our front living room in Beaver Mountain, my dad eventually started a little grocery store in Stigler. And that's what we were doing for a number of years. When I was twelve or thirteen, he taught me to drive an old '36 Ford that we had; and I would deliver groceries for people from the grocery store. In that small town many people walked to the store, but they'd buy a whole bunch of groceries and I'd haul them back to their home. We also sold hundred-pound bags of feed out of the back door of the store. I found that a hundred-pound bag of feed would fit between the hood and the fender. I could even take two at a time. I don't remember if I lifted them, but I got them where they were supposed to go.

Dad put in a complete meat market and became the butcher. He built a pretty good business but it was a credit business which is doomed to failure because people don't pay their bills. It wound up that he had a whole box full of uncollected receivables. He also had his own debts to the grocery wholesale houses. But those debts ran for two or three years until he was able to pay every one of the suppliers off.

I wrote this in the 1960s about my father:

> DEFINITION OF A REAL MAN: One who has confidence, but does not show it, one who can be courteous in the face of discourtesy, one who keeps his word, his temper, and his friends. One who wins respect by being respectable and respectful. One who has a steady eye, a steady nerve, a steady tongue and steady habits. One who is silent when he has nothing to say. One who is calm when he judges and humble when he misjudged. That defines a real man and a gentleman, and by these standards my father was indeed a "Real Man."

Me at about fifteen years of age in Clovis, New Mexico—the earliest picture of myself I could find.

We used to have a few milk cows. It was my job to milk them in the morning, drive them to the pasture where they would graze during the day and bring them back to the barn for their evening milking. Usually with a herd of cows, there is a leader. If you can get the leader to go in the direction you want, the rest will usually follow. The leader of our herd was always ready to go back to the barn in the evening, but would sometimes get distracted and begin to wander off the path. I learned that if I followed right behind the herd, I could get the lead cow back on the path by chucking a rock to her right if she was veering right, or one to the left if she veered left. I would follow behind letting her take the lead, and with a few choice tosses, I could drive the entire herd. In looking back, I think that is a way to manage people, let them go where they know they want to go, and occasionally toss a comment, or a question, or a compliment their way to make sure they are staying on the path.

When we moved to Stigler and my mother went to enroll me in school, she told them I belonged in the sixth grade, even though I had only completed fourth grade at Beaver Mountain. Mrs. Willowby was my teacher and Mrs. Carlin was the principal of the grade school. Mrs. Willowby's husband was in the military, and I guess the first time I ever really paid any attention to geography was her showing us on a map where her husband was fighting during the Second World War.

I hadn't really learned much at the school on Beaver Mountain and I guess since I had skipped fifth grade, I had not really learned to read. It wasn't too far into the year and we were reading a story in class and everyone was taking turns at reading a paragraph. The story was coming around the room, approaching me, and I was just scared to death because I knew I didn't know how to read. But as people were reading, I knew I could follow where they were in the book. It dawned on me that I could reason out what those words were. So when it came my turn, I stammered through my paragraph about as well as anyone else did. That's the day I went home and said, "I think I may have learned to read today."

Even today, reading is my favorite pastime. I enjoy reading biographies, history, fiction and personal development books.

I went to junior high in the seventh grade. There were grades seven, eight, nine, ten, eleven and twelve—all in the same building. Now what was I learning in school? Not much.

I did get something out of the English classes. Part of an assignment was memorizing a poem and I devised a system that worked pretty well.

I took any poem no matter how long it was and I'd say to myself the first line of the poem, and then look away and when I could say that first line perfectly then I'd look at the second line, and then I'd put the two together and add another line. Pretty soon I'd be reciting two or three verses without any break at all. I can still recite many poems from memory. My favorites are "Invictus," "The Homebuilder's Prayer," "Little Boy Blue," "Alumnus Football," and "A Reluctant Investor's Lament."

MANY YEARS LATER, I taught my two little daughters to do that when they were going to a private school in El Paso, Texas. Kristel was seven years old and came home upset and said, "I'm supposed to have a poem in school tomorrow. And I don't know one."

Joy, my wife, was preparing supper and said to me, "Jack, you know how to memorize a poem, please go in and help her."

We had about forty-five minutes together. She's a sharp little gal. By the time Joy called us into supper, she asked, "How are you coming on the poem?" And I said, "I think she's got it."

And Kristel stood up and said, "Invictus by William Ernest Henley" and recited the entire thing. Joy dropped her spatula. Kristel can still recite that poem today. She got an A+. Kiana, our granddaughter, memorized that poem as well in less than forty-five minutes.

Me with daughters Kristel and Monica around the time Kristel was learning how to memorize Invictus.

Invictus

by William Ernest Henley

Out of the night that covers me,
Black as the pit from pole to pole,
I thank whatever gods may be
For my unconquerable soul.

In the fell clutch of circumstance
I have not winced nor cried aloud.
Beneath the bludgeonings of chance
My head is bloody, but unbowed.

Beyond this place of wrath and tears
Looms but the Horror of the shade,
And yet the menace of the years
Finds and shall find me unafraid.

It matters not how strait the gate,
How charged with punishments the scroll,
I am the master of my fate:
I am the captain of my soul.

They did not coddle the children in school in my day. In study hall there was a guy named Jimmy Spears. He was a mean kid who was always in trouble. For a while all the kids had long tubes and would blow things through them. One day I was sitting there supposedly reading and I felt something hit me on the neck. It was a spitball. I looked around and there was Jimmy Spears, just grinning from ear to ear. I knew what he had done.

So I loaded me up a spitball and got all ready and everything. And I spit it. Then I happened to look up. Standing at the entrance to the study hall was the principal of the school, Mr. Kirkpatrick. It's the second guy that always gets caught. He was motioning to me with one finger. So I get up and go with him, knowing exactly what was going to happen. And I went into his office and he said, "I don't think we have to discuss anything. You know what the problem is."

He grabbed me by the back of my pants and pulled them just as tight as he could over my little old butt and took the paddle he kept handy in his office. I don't know how many licks it was, but it wasn't pleasant.

I put many thousands of miles on the motor scooter I acquired. This was the one I had bought with the money I got from selling my horse Danny, who was bought with my pig profits. It had a Briggs & Stratton engine that could get up to twenty-five or thirty miles an hour on a paved street. It had a box on the front, so I'd use that to make money, transporting things around for people, including deliveries for my dad.

My sisters did not work in the store. I think my dad felt that a male was expected to perform and make a living someday and females were going to get married. So learning how to work fell a lot more in my area than in my sisters'.

I made some friends in Stigler, and we ran together, but we didn't call it a gang in those days. There were four or five of us who spent a lot of time together. My best buddy was Lyle Redding, a very attractive little fellow who moved to Stigler when his parents were transferred there. His father was an official with the coal company or something. Actually it was his stepdad. His mother was divorced and had remarried.

There was a bully named Ernest. He was one of two kids of a single father and as is often the case, he was pretty maladjusted. He had a chip on his shoulder; I mean he was just a mean kid. At a Boy Scout meeting one evening, when the Scoutmaster didn't show up, which was often the case, Ernest started picking on everybody. When he came to Lyle

Redding, Lyle told him outright, "Ernest, don't try to pull that crap on me. I don't go for it." Ernest said, "Yeah, yeah." And Lyle Redding popped him in the face just as hard as he could with his fist, knocked him on the ground, jumped right on top of him and while sitting on him, started hitting him. Left, right, left, right, beating him in the face. Everybody was really surprised; no one had ever dealt with Ernest in that manner before. So naturally Lyle sort of became my hero. It changed Ernest's life a little bit, too. He wasn't the same kind of a bully after that.

There was one girl in the seventh or eighth grade who developed a little quicker than the other girls and she ran with us just like one of the boys. You've got all the merry men over here but the leader of the pack was Lyle Redding and his right hand assistant was Charlene Meadows. They were like Robin Hood and Maid Marian. She had dark black hair, wore black horn-rimmed glasses and then from the neck down, you would definitely have had to notice her.

We rode bikes. The little town of Whitefield, Oklahoma, was six miles away. Sundays we'd get on our bicycles even though I had a motor scooter. I rode my bicycle like the rest of the kids, and we rode them all the way over to Whitefield and we'd go to the country store and have a Coke or something and come on back. We'd stop along the way where there was a little cave about fifty yards off the highway and we'd stop and go sit in this little old cave for a while. There was no such thing as any serious mischief then, so there was no supervision. There was a movie theater in Stigler where I went to see Roy Rogers, Gene Autry, Lash LaRue and other cowboy movie stars every time they were showing.

Bell Drug Store was an old fashion drug store in Stigler with the long counter and stools and I decided to blow thirty cents one day and go order a milkshake. They sent this thing down to me. It was a great big glass full of milkshake and a metal can with the excess from when they made it. They always did that. And I put that straw in that thing and I took the first slurp. I absolutely thought I had died and gone to heaven it was so wonderful tasting, and I still enjoy a milkshake today. Chocolate, just like the first one I had. The best milkshake is at Whataburger.

I take those home and what I don't drink I set in the fridge and take a little sip of it from time to time until it is all gone.

"The best way *to kill time is to work it to death.*"

—Henri Matisse

Five

The Great White Hunter

Although I didn't enjoy school in Stigler all that much, that didn't keep me from trying to impress the teachers. Mrs. Ulum was the English teacher, she was a widow, and she had a grown son named Glenn, who lived in Oklahoma City. She would tell us about him sometimes. When she punished someone, she'd say, "Give me your hand." She'd take their hand and beat it with a ruler.

I sat in the front seat and contrived to become the teacher's pet, and I succeeded. She was my buddy. So I decided to get her a gift. I didn't realize it at the time, but getting that gift would forever change my attitude about adventure in the great outdoors. My dad and my brother-in-law were going duck hunting one weekend and I went with them. Although I wasn't much of a duck hunter, I got them to agree that if we got any ducks, I could have one of them and take it to Mrs. Ulum.

Turns out we had every possible kind of problem you could imagine. We got in the Canadian River at Whitefield and we were going to float down to Fordam in a rubber raft about fifteen miles and have someone pick us up. Well, the weather turned very bad and it started raining and blowing and we never did make it to Fordam. We finally left the rubber raft we were in and started walking and came upon a little old house. This must have been ten or eleven o'clock at night; this whole thing was supposed to have been over by five-thirty or six.

I was cold and hungry, and we had only brought enough for lunch. So we got to this house and it was the poorest family you ever saw. My dad said, "We'll pay you, but we need some food." And they checked and looked and they came back and said the only thing they had in the place was one can of tomatoes. They opened that can of tomatoes and I ate a little bit of it. They had an old beat up car and they agreed to take us to Stigler. My dad said, "I'll be glad to pay you for the ride." They came to the grocery store a few days later, and my dad let them load up on groceries and said, "Take them. They're free."

That same day, a horrible electrical storm hit the whole area, and ducks, which were attempting to fly south, got lost and disoriented and were just landing, some crashing, all over the streets in Stigler. Even though we had not shot a duck from the hunting trip, I picked up a duck off the street for Mrs. Ulum. I took it to her and she said, "I already have three others."

Much later in life, I had one other hunting experience that again has not endeared me to that lifestyle. One of the presidents of a bank that we did business with, Bob Payne of El Paso Federal, and a friend of his, wanted to go hunting for Sandhill Cranes at El Fuerte, Mexico. It was a huge farming area that had belonged to William Randolph Hearst. I had a plane and a pilot license, so I flew them down there and we landed on this little old rough strip. It's a wonder the airplane even held up. And in addition I was sick with a terrible cold.

We went out in the afternoon when we got there and set up in some hunting blinds. I was huddled with them and suddenly we heard "honk, honk." I knew the cranes were coming. Bob told me they are very intelligent birds and that if they see you or see any movement, they will turn and fly in the opposite direction. So be very still; don't move and don't say anything.

He raised up carefully, looked over the edge of this blind and said, "Okay they're coming towards us. They're coming towards us." Then finally he said, "Let's jump up and shoot as many as we can." We jump up and go bam, bam, bam. Bob was a skeet shooting champion and these giant twenty-five pound birds start dropping all around us, flop, flop, flop.

So we gather all the cranes and put them in the van that brought us out there. We're two or three miles from where we're supposed to be staying in this farm. And then it started raining and the van got stuck and we tried every way under the sun to get it moving and we couldn't. We wound up spending the night in that van with a bunch of twenty-five pound dead birds. My hunting experiences have not been the best.

In his message "Greener Pastures," Earl Nightingale tells the story of a farmer in Africa who sold his farm to go search for diamonds. The person who bought the farm ended up having one of the richest diamond mines in the world. The moral is that we are all sitting in our own acres of diamonds, if we could just see them.

PART II

Creativity

God thought the earth into existence and we can all do the same thing with our thoughts. Again, "whatever the mind of man can conceive and believe, it can achieve." We become what we think about.

Six

Picking Weeds in Clovis, New Mexico

In 1948, when I was approaching age fifteen, we moved to Clovis, New Mexico. We moved because my father could not make it in the grocery business. Many of his customers bought on credit, and then didn't pay their bills. Then they would not shop at my Dad's store anymore. They would shop at the other stores even though they had to pay cash. He was not collecting enough on the grocery bills that people owed him. It got so bad that Dad did not have enough money to pay his suppliers, and he was looking to start over again in another town.

The only reason we chose Clovis was because of my sister Louise. She had married a fellow at the end of World War II named Omer Clarkson. He went to college in Stillwater, Oklahoma, got a degree in meteorology and went to work for the federal government, eventually spending forty years working as a weatherman. Around 1947 they sent him to Walker Air Force Base in Roswell, New Mexico, to be a weatherman.

So my folks would travel from Stigler to Roswell for a visit. They wound up spending the night several times in Clovis on their way. They were attracted to the area for some reason, and some relatives lived in Clovis, including Aunt Jenny Norris. They decided that's where we were going to go. They said, "Let's go and see what we can find in Clovis." Doctors also thought the drier air of New Mexico would be good for my father's respiratory problems that were beginning to surface.

I didn't know that much about our business trouble, but I did get word that we were moving to Clovis. I remember going to Mr. Head's drugstore and saying, "Oh we're going to be moving and I don't know what to think about it."

He said, "Where are you going?" I said, "Clovis, New Mexico." And he said, "Oh I've been through there on vacation. It's a nice little town. You'll like it." That was the first encouraging news I had about Clovis.

When we moved to Clovis in 1948, just before my sophomore year of high school, the population was about eleven or twelve thousand people. My father got a job selling meat for a local meatpacker and my mother got a job as a checker in a small local grocery store and we all worked except my sister Becky. She was too young. Bette worked at the Clovis National Bank.

I got a job that summer setting pins at a bowling alley. That was before the Brunswick automatic setters. I got good enough that I could operate two or three alleys at once. You had to jump and move pretty fast but you got paid five cents a line for each alley that you set. There should have been combat pay as well since some mean teenagers used to try to hit me with their bowling balls while I was setting the pins. I would ride my bicycle home from work, about three miles away, at eleven-thirty or twelve o'clock at night after the bowling alley closed. When school started, I had to quit.

Then my mother heard about another job at Harry Lyman's floral shop. Harry was a gruff old boy. When I went to the shop he stood there and looked at me, "What do you want kid?"

I was scared to death of him. "I-I-I heard you might be looking for a boy to work."

"Do you know how to work?"

"Yessir."

"Are you sure you can do it?"

"Yessir."

"Okay. Come to work tomorrow. I'm going to pay you fifty cents an hour. Can you get here by four o'clock every day?"

"Yessir."

"You'll work from four to six and then on Saturdays you work ten hours."

They had a worker named Bud Stebbins who had been there for quite some time. Harry said to Bud, "Take him out and give him something to do, Bud."

He goes out, hands me a tin can and we go out to the greenhouse. These greenhouses were close to a hundred feet long with elevated flower beds—beds and beds and beds of carnations, all in rows about four feet wide, running the length of the greenhouse.

Bud said, "Here's what I want you to do. Pick these weeds out and put them in that can." So he went along ten feet, picking about two feet into the bed, showing me what to do. He said, "You got it?" and I said, "Yessiree."

He gives me the can and leaves. I did as was shown, and picked about two feet into the bed. He comes back in an hour and a half and I'm way down at the other end. There is a strip running down the middle for the full length of the bed that still has weeds. He said, "What are you doing?"

I said, "I'm doing exactly what you showed me to do."

"Well you idiot, didn't you think that those weeds out in the middle had to be picked too?" So he showed me, and I went down the other side and picked those weeds out too.

That was a lesson. It helped me understand when new people come to work they don't know shit from wild honey. They are lost and what might be obvious to you is not always obvious to others. It means you have to be patient with them. It doesn't necessarily mean they are dumb.

In the summer time, to keep the greenhouse cool you had to go up and put whitewash on the glass roof. During the winter and fall it rained enough to wash it off so that the greenhouse could get the solar heat. One day they had me up painting on the greenhouse roof and I lost my balance and fell through two panes of glass twenty feet to a flower bed. I broke my arm when I hit it on one of the braces. They took me to the hospital, but I started back to work again as soon as I could.

I wound up working at Lyman's Flowers from my sophomore year nearly through graduation for fifty cents an hour. That worked out to about ten dollars a week during the school year. Five dollars of that I brought home and turned over to my parents to help pay the cost of running the house. The other five I spent on shoes and socks and shirts. Today, parents think that kids have to have an allowance. Mine was a reverse allowance, so every week I gave money to my parents.

"*Every adversity carries with it the seed of an equivalent or greater benefit.*"

—Napoleon Hill

Seven

Stage Struck

When I got to Clovis ready to start my sophomore year in high school, the registrar said, "Okay, in this high school there are three possibilities. You can take the agricultural route or you can take the shop and auto mechanics route or you can take the academic route."

And I said, "I don't have any intention of being a farmer or an auto mechanic so I guess I'll take the academic route."

And they said, "One of the things you have to have is two years of a foreign language." The possibilities were French, Latin or Spanish, so I inquired of the other students which one was easiest and they said, oh Spanish is definitely easier.

So I took two years of high school Spanish and had no problem with it. I also had twenty hours of Spanish in college. Everything in Spanish seemed reasonable and logical. I did well in it at college and even today, I'm pretty fluent and have had many opportunities to use my Spanish.

A man answered an ad for a bilingual speaker and assured the employer that he was bilingual. When he began work, they found he couldn't speak any Spanish. When questioned about it, he said, "Sure I'm bilingual. I speak English and German."

The person who helped me most when I started at Clovis High School was Jimmy Griggs. I met Jimmy through my Aunt Jenny Norris who also lived in Clovis. Her husband had been my Uncle Dick Norris, my grandmother's brother, who was kind of a legend in the family. Everybody called him Uncle Dick and he was an outstanding guy. He spoke Spanish and owned an airplane in the 1930s.

He was a great trader and bought sheep and wool from all the ranchers around Santa Rosa and Las Vegas, New Mexico. It was a big deal when he came to visit these isolated ranches. Most of these ranchers had never flown in a plane, much less had someone land a private plane on their ranch. He'd spend the night at the ranch. He had a personal relationship with all his customers. They'd come into the Moise Brothers Trading Post where he worked, and buy all their supplies for all year long. He'd help them in marketing their sheep and their wool and they'd pay their bills and start all over again.

Uncle Dick made a big impression on me as well. When I was four or five years old I had a jelly jar that was shaped like Porky Pig and designed to be used as a bank once the jelly was gone. It had a lid that screwed on and a little slit to put money through. That was my first place to save money, long before my leather pouch. A great big event occurred when Uncle Dick came to Oklahoma to visit relatives. He stayed at my grandmother's for a day or so and my folks brought all the kids down to see the great hero Uncle Dick Norris.

He put me up on his knee and asked, "You have a piggy bank?"

"Yeah," I said.

"Can I see it?" he said.

It happened to be at my grandmother's house. She told me where it was and I went and got it and showed it to him. He took it and fished in his pocket and brought out the biggest coin I had ever seen in my life: a silver fifty-cent piece.

He said, "Let's see if I can put this through that slot." But the slot wasn't big enough.

He said, "Oh gee, I was going to put this in your piggy bank, but I guess I can't." And he started to put it back in his pocket.

"Oh no," I thought, "I'm going to lose this opportunity of a lifetime."

But he smiled and took the coin out. "I'm just kidding." he said. He screwed the top off the piggy bank and put the fifty-cent piece in it. I felt like I owned Fort Knox.

Uncle Dick died some years later. His widow, Aunt Jenny, lived at Tenth and Main in Clovis, where they had had a home together. She had a vacant lot next door. Shortly after our move to Clovis, she came to see us.

"Jack, I want to know if I can hire you to do something for me?" she said.

"Sure, what do you need?"

"I need you to get the weeds cleared up on my vacant lot next door to my house."

"Oh you bet."

So I showed up the next morning at seven o'clock and said, "I'm here to work." She gave me a hoe and a rake and I went to work. She would come out every hour or so and say, "You'd better slow down. Here's some iced tea. You should come over here and sit in the shade." She was so nice and so sweet and she said, "You know you have a cousin living here by the name of Jimmy Griggs."

"Really"

"Yeah, he's a very nice young man, he's one year older than you. I'm going to get in touch with him and ask him to come over and meet you." So I was at Aunt Jenny's house working on the lot, and this good-looking slim, sleek young fellow comes zooming up on his motor scooter and went into Aunt Jenny's house. She came out with him and said, "Jack this is your cousin Jimmy Griggs" and he said, "Well you want to go riding around and I'll show you the town?"

I said, "No, I can't. I'm working on Aunt Jenny's vacant lot."

And she said, "Oh no no no, you go."

So I spent that first summer running around with Jimmy Griggs. And then when school started I learned he was the absolute hero of the school. He was the star basketball player, even as a sophomore, and a track star like Jim Thorpe had been in Oklahoma. I remember one track meet when I went out to run the mile. It was a regional meet held at Eastern New Mexico University with schools from all over sending people to compete. Clovis won the track meet and Jimmy Griggs won first place in the one hundred yard dash, the 220 yard low hurdles, the 220 yard high hurdles, the high jump, the broad jump and the pole vault. I think Clovis accumulated thirty-eight points to win the overall track meet and Jimmy Griggs was responsible for twenty-nine of them.

He had a younger sister. She was one year behind me. She and I started becoming big buddies.

> *There is the story of the handsome prince who asked the beautiful princess to marry him. She said no, and he lived happily ever after.*

I never considered myself particularly athletic. I hadn't found my spot in school, but the junior play came along and so I thought why not?, and I tried out and got a part. One of the gals in our choral group, Dela Ruth, was a year ahead of me. She was blond and playful, and she would catch me back behind the curtain for a quick kiss. I guess I was pretty dumb because I wasn't real sure what her intentions were.

One of the plays we did was called *I Remember Mama*, and we did *Our Town* as a senior. I played Dr. Wilson in *I Remember Mama*. In the play this family had come from Norway to the United States and they were very poor and they all worked very hard and Mama, the grandmother, supposedly had quite a fortune. They went through every kind of hardship you can imagine, but they always got through and kept saying let's hold off and we can tap into mama's bank account if we get past this one thing. And at the end, they found out that her bank account had $3.29 in it. But it's the thought of what might have been in there that kept them going.

Years later I heard a story that reminded me of the same thing. There was a very successful man who was approached by a young man who asked him the secret of his success. The successful man gave him a small box and told him he should carry it to his business three times every day. He was also told to never look in the box. He followed the instructions religiously and after several years he was tremendously successful. He returned the box to the man who had given it to him and who was very old by then. He told the man, "This has worked so well for me that it would only be fair for me to return it so that you may give it to someone else. But please unlock the box and let me see what is really inside." The old wise man, opened the box and it was completely empty. It was not the contents of the box that made the young man successful. It was going to check his business three times a day that caused the success, plus the belief that he had the key to success in his possession.

The longer I live, the more I realize the impact of attitude on life. Earl Nightingale called attitude the magic word. He said if we have a good attitude, we will get good results, a fair attitude will bring us fair results and a bad attitude will bring us bad results.

Eight

Not So Easy Reading

Everyone at Clovis High was assigned to a homeroom. Our homeroom teacher was a single lady named Lucille Buchanan. She was the sweetest nicest lady and took an interest in all the students in her class. Miss Buchanan must have done something right, because the kids in her homeroom went on to truly impressive careers.

There was an English teacher named Mrs. Putnam, and she was absolutely terrific. We just had a rapport. The first book I really liked was *The Sea-Wolf* by Jack London. It told the story of hardship overcome and success achieved. She required us to read Chaucer and *Paradise Lost* by John Milton and two or three Shakespeare plays. She was really fantastic.

Because of Mrs. Putnam I loved the classics, especially *Paradise Lost*. Considering John Milton was blind when he wrote that book is just amazing.

I was in awe of the understanding of nature and of man that Shakespeare had and the appropriateness, even today, of things that he wrote. I still use some of his lines today: "The lady doth protest too much, me thinks" and "Et tu, Brute?"

Picnic at Wanda King's family farm outside of Clovis, summer of 1949.
Top photo—*Me and Jim Whatley*
Bottom photo—*Clockwise from bottom left: Me, kneeling, Jim Whatley, Art Snipes, and batter Donald Todd.*

I read all kinds of other books as well. The geometry teacher, Mr. Norman, told us one day in class that we should read a book called *How to Win Friends and Influence People* by Dale Carnegie. I rushed to the library to be sure and get a copy before anyone else beat me to it. It turned out I was the first one to check out that book in three years, but I was certainly able to use the lessons taught by Mr. Carnegie when I was selling meat, or shoes, or houses later in life. I learned to treat every person I meet as if they are the most important person in the world.

At one point, all the boys in school were getting Mohawk haircuts, and then they also started bleaching their hair to a dirty yellow, and I did that too. At the end of an English class one day, Mrs. Putnam said, "Jack, I want to see you." When everybody left, she came over to me and looked me right in the eye and said, "I am so disappointed in you." I said, "Why?" And she said, "Because all these other kids can do all these silly stupid things, but I just expect more than that of you."

My friends and I were awfully good kids by today's standards. Nobody smoked; nobody drank beer. I heard there were two or three guys who had gone out and gotten a hold of some beer somehow and drank it and frankly those were not my kind of people. I didn't want to have anything more to do with them after that. We always went out on picnics to people's ranches and farms. We played baseball and looked at the girls. And we went to church every Sunday.

This little town of Clovis had some of the early street paving done with bricks. From the railroad depot up through the first eight blocks, Main Street had brick pavers, and that's where all the businesses were. A favorite pastime was to get a hold of the family car, or if you owned one that was even better, and load it up with your friends and drag Main. Back and forth, back and forth, back and forth waving and making obscene gestures every time you saw someone that you knew. I have spent countless hours and days dragging Main. It must be something about that small town, but my kids did it too. And their kids who grew up in Clovis did it as well. Go figure.

Me in 1953—my senior year of high school.

Once I was old enough, I always owned a car of some kind. During the summer time, Mr. Lyman let me work all day, every day. That was when most of the flower-raising business was done anyway. I would work pretty much all day at fifty cents an hour and make twenty-five dollars a week. It didn't take me too long to put a couple hundred dollars down on a $1,100 car and make payments on it. I had an old cream-colored Oldsmobile Hydroflow. It was a good old car; it worked well.

When I was still in high school, I took a summer off from working for Lyman's and went to work for Montgomery Ward because they were paying nearly twenty cents more per hour. But the great deal was that my supervisor, Mr. Strickler, paid me fifty dollars to distribute sales flyers two days a month. I figured out how to hire two guys for two days, paying ten dollars each to hang the flyers on the doors of homes. I drove back and forth in my old Oldsmobile all loaded down with those flyers, keeping my two workers stocked with flyers while they walked from house to house. I would clear thirty dollars for myself. So in high school in addition to working at Lyman's Flowers I would take off from school, missing a couple of days a month and distribute Montgomery Ward's flyers. I guess I put more energy into making money than making grades.

The most valuable thing about my high school experience was developing a circle of great friends. Starting with the twenty-fifth anniversary of our graduation, I have been going regularly to the class reunions. There were 123 students that graduated in 1951 and a while back we had fifty people show up for the reunion.

> *I was once an emcee for the class reunion and I found this story to tell. Dr. Bill Hale, the husband of one of our classmates, is an ear, nose and throat specialist. I said: Dr. Hale has his office in a high-rise building and every afternoon he comes down and gets off the elevator and walks across the lobby to a little cantina. The bartender, named Richard but everybody calls him Dick, knows what he's going to order. He orders an almond daiquiri and always sits at the same barstool.*
>
> *So they have a little game. When the elevator door opens and he sees Dr. Hale coming, he quickly tries to make that daiquiri and have it sitting at the right place by the time he gets there.*
>
> *One day, he's doing really well but he picks up his almond shaker and it's empty. He picks up a hickory nut shaker and sprinkles it on quickly and sets it down just as*

> *Dr. Hale's butt hits the stool. He picks it up, takes a small sip and says, "Is this an almond daiquiri, Dick?"*
> *He said, "No, it's a hickory daiquiri, Doc."*

My class was pretty remarkable. Johnny Sieren went to law school then practiced law in Dallas for twenty-nine years, I believe. Then he became a judge and served on the bench for an additional fifteen years or so. Three classmates became doctors; there were a couple of lawyers. There were just some really outstanding people in Miss Buchanan's homeroom, and I think she had a lot to do with that. Art and Wanda Snipes were also in that homeroom.

Art and Wanda Snipes have been married for sixty years, and at the last high school reunion, in Albuquerque, New Mexico, I asked, "What is the secret of your marriage, Art?" and he said, "Jack we're still waiting to see if it's going to work out."

Bill and Sue Hale are good friends. Bill, the well-known ear, nose and throat specialist, has practiced for forty years in Amarillo, Texas, and Sue was one of my best buddies in high school. We never were boyfriend and girlfriend; it was a true platonic relationship. We took classes together and studied together, and we did some homework when I went to her house. I remember figuring out the difference between carnivorous and herbivorous during one study session. At least I learned that much in high school.

School is a place where one can learn a lot, but also a place where one can make really good lifelong friends.

Attitude, to me, is more important than facts. It is more important than the past, than education, than money, than circumstances, than failures, than success, than what other people think or say or do.

Nine

Wedding Bells

I WASN'T MUCH OF A STUDENT, but going to college appealed to me. Mom and Dad didn't finish high school but I went to college because that was what everyone was doing. Several of my friends went to Eastern New Mexico University (ENMU), a small college in Portales, New Mexico, about nineteen miles from Clovis. We used to think that it was really something but it only had about three thousand students. Today it has about 5,500.

I started college in 1951. My college studies didn't work out particularly well. Within a few weeks of starting at the University, I got a job working at Hatch Packing Company in Portales. I would go out there as soon as I finished my classes every day and usually worked in the sausage kitchen with a fellow named Charlie Malone.

Part of my job was to stay and clean the place and steam the stainless steel tables and the floor after everyone had gone home. I would miss dinner every evening at the chow hall. Jack Murphy, my roommate and friend from Clovis, would bring a tray of food and keep it in the dorm so when I got home from the Hatch Packing Company at eight-thirty or nine at night, I could eat some dinner.

I made excellent grades in Spanish, but overall I didn't do so well. I remember one geography class in particular. I wore a tie to school one day, just for kind of a joke, and Professor Rowen said, "Jack, I'm so surprised to see you wearing a tie. I love that tie." I said, "Here it goes, Sir, it's yours." I thought I had the professor lined up, but my relationship with him wasn't as good as I thought it was because I got a D in his class.

> *A boy leaves home and goes away and his family doesn't hear from him for about five years. Then they get an envelope with a gold embossed return address to Willie Washington, BS. They read the letter and he tells them everything's fine. The wife looks at the husband and says, "What do you reckon that BS stands for?" He said, "Now come on, woman. Everybody knows what that is. That stands for Bull Shit."*
>
> *Two years later, they get another letter from Willie; this time, Willie Washington BS, MS. And the wife says, "Well, you done told me what that BS stands for, but what do you suppose that MS means?" And the dad says, "More of the Same."*
>
> *Then a couple years later still, they get another letter from Willie Washington signed Willie Washington, BS, MS, PhD. And the wife says, "Okay, Mr. Wise Guy. Can you tell me what that means?" He said, "Sure. That means Piled Higher and Deeper."*

I left Hatch Packing Company at the end of the school year and worked with my father during the summer. In the fall, I started school again but I was living in Clovis and driving back and forth to Portales. I usually carpooled with someone, but after only a few weeks, I decided

Lunell Harrington. This photo was taken close to the time when we were married in 1953.

to quit, which I did in the fall of 1952 and went to work full time in my father's meat packing company, Rancho Packing Company. I also became more involved with Lunell Harrington, who would become my first wife.

I met Lunell dragging Main in Clovis. She was still a senior in high school and I was in my first year in college. She was an only daughter, had two brothers. Her father was a well-to-do farmer. They had money and new cars and they had just moved to Clovis from Hollene, a little farming community thirty miles north of Clovis. They had turned a practically new car over to her, and she would be dragging Main with a bunch of girlfriends.

I would be dragging Main with some guys, including Jerry Roberts (who became an OB-GYN specialist and moved to Colorado Springs, Colorado, and practiced there for forty years, recently deceased). Jerry was valedictorian of our high school class and very intelligent and he said, "Jack, you have to pay attention to that girl in the Mercury that we keep meeting."

"Why?"

"Because, she looks at you every time."

I said, "Well let's find out who she is."

And the next day he said, "I found out her name is Harrington and she lives at 116 West Manana."

"Jerry, how did you find that out?"

"Well I wrote the license number down and I checked out who owned the car. And I already called her and told her you are interested in her. She's expecting a call."

I called her, took her to a movie and one thing led to another.

In May of 1953 we got married. We lived in an upstairs efficiency apartment and she worked for the KCLV radio station in Clovis.

Lunell and my engagement picture.

One night a woman woke up and discovered her husband was not in bed. She started walking through the house and heard whimpering coming from the kitchen. She found her husband sitting at the table with his head in his hands crying. She said, "What's wrong, honey?" He said, "Do you remember that time your father found us in the back seat of my car and he told me to either marry you or I would go to jail for twenty years?" She said, "Yes I remember." He said, "I would be getting out today," and continued crying.

I was working at my father's packing plant, doing everything, but mostly selling. We only served Portales and Clovis and our customers were grocery stores and restaurants. Everything was wholesale. We supplied them with everything, and we slaughtered cattle and pigs and offered all kinds of items that you make from them. We fabricated meat for restaurants, sold steaks pre-cut and pre-made to restaurants, along with lots of hamburger meat. In fact my father would go to local sales and buy bulls because of their leanness and the fact that they were so tough that without boning and grinding the meat, they weren't edible anyway. So we bought lots of bulls and turned it into hamburger meat and sold it to all the restaurants.

I became pretty good with a knife and learned all the intricacies of meat cutting. Every part of a cow, bull and steer, and every part of a pig, I got to know intimately. I've got a few little scars too. I almost cut my index finger off on a Biro meat saw. For a few years, the scars showed up bright and purple. I was kind of proud of that but they've all blended in now and you'd have to have a really good light to see how the doctor sewed it back together. The doctor said, "I don't know if the joint is going to work." But he made it work pretty well.

Then I lost the end of my little finger on my right hand. I took it to the doctor and asked, "Is there anything you can do to make this grow back?" He said, "I don't think so." But he took it and put it on the end of my finger and put a bandage around it nice and tight and said, "Now don't take this off for a week or ten days and then come back and see me."

When I came back he said, "Son of a gun, this seems to be growing back on." Most of my cuts were on my left hand because I am right handed. And I'd cut myself with the right hand most of the time. I soon came to realize that the meat packing business wasn't all it was "cut out" to be.

Our surroundings, our environment, our circumstances, our relationships are a mirror of our attitude. If we want a change in any of these, we must first make a change in our attitude.

This photo was taken at the end of basic training after I was drafted into the Army.

Ten

In the Army

In 1953, soon after I settled down with my bride, Lunell, I was drafted into the Army. I tried to think of every excuse to keep me from going into the Army, including claiming that Lunell was pregnant, even though she wasn't. I tell people about my army career and I say, "If you'll look carefully at the corner of Fifth and Mitchell in Clovis, where the old post office used to be, you'll find two heel marks on the sidewalk. That's where they loaded me on the bus to go to the Army."

I took basic training at Fort Bliss, in El Paso, Texas, and I had eight weeks of infantry training and eight weeks of radar operator training. Upon completion of this training, they sent our group to all kinds of places. I didn't realize it until I worked in personnel and had access to my files, that my records showed I had an IQ of 142. Only one guy in the entire battalion of one thousand men had one higher than me. Still I wasn't smart enough to stay out of the Army.

When the orders came out, there were twenty-three of us, as I recall, going from Fort Bliss to Fort Lewis, Washington, for reassignment. And we were to take a train. There were travel vouchers and there was an asterisk by my name and next to the asterisk it said the group leader. When we got together to board the train, I said, "Fellows, I don't have any idea why I'm the group leader according to these orders we all have, but let me tell you right now, I'm not planning to wet-nurse any of you. If any of you get off the train at any stop and don't get back on, I'll only report that you're absent without leave and they'll send the Feds out after you. I'm not going to act as a group leader other than to say you'd better be responsible for yourselves, period."

Light travels faster than sound. This is why some people appear bright until you hear them speak.

We all got there in good shape. They split us up and sent groups to three different places. I was sent out to Camp Hanford, Washington, and it was in December, freezing cold. We stood outside with our duffle bags, waiting for something and it happened that a warrant officer opened a door to a building and stuck his head out and said, "Any of you guys know how to type?"

There were three of us who held our hands up. The first guy went in for the interview and I talked to the other one who happened to be from Albuquerque, named Joe. I said, "How fast do you type, Joe?"

He said, "I don't know, about 110 words a minute."

"And what is your profession in civilian life?"

He said, "I'm a concert pianist."

Anyway I was the last one to be interviewed. When Mr. Fry, the warrant officer, interviewed me, he asked: "How fast do you type?"

"Well sir when I was in high school, I typed about forty-three words per minute."

"And how many mistakes?"

"Five."

"Think you'd like to work in personnel?"

"Yes sir."

"Go get your duffle bag. You've got the job."

"What about the guy from Albuquerque who can type 110 words a minute?"

"Why that guy's as different as a three dollar bill. I wouldn't have him on the place."

It was a terrible thing to say, but his prejudice landed me the job working in personnel. What a wonderful deal that was—instead of going out into the boondocks to sit on a radar van with 120-millimeter guns with live ammo protecting the Hanford Atomic Works, which is scattered up and down the Columbia River, I got an office job in personnel.

I didn't relate to some of the others I was stationed with. The guys would all go out partying. I went out a few times with some of the guys. I recall a dance someplace. One of the guys was a big old husky guy named Henry Norton, but everybody called him Honk. He was from Arizona. Turns out he had a weekend job as a bouncer in one of the places where the dances took place. I didn't get a thrill out of going out—it was a lot of noise, a lot of chaos. I had no interest in partying. I had always worked, and I just hated wasting time. In the evenings I concentrated on reading good books and listening to classical music.

They eventually put me in a little two-man cubicle with two beds and a roommate. My roommate was partying all the time, so I had the place to myself weekends. I took some saved funds and purchased a Webcor phonograph and some highbrow records. So I read books and listened to classical music every weekend. I liked Mozart best of all but I only had two records.

As it turned out, having the time to reflect really paid off. I read quite a few books. One book in particular had a big impact on me—*Return to Religion* by Dr. Henry C. Link. In the book, he wrote that while he was at Yale, he lost his faith. A lot of religious teaching seemed like a bunch of bull to him. But years later, while he was raising his children, he realized that his family needed some sort of core values to hang onto, and so he raised them in the church. He was able to ignore all the bad stuff and just focus on the good.

I had begun to question some of the stories in the Bible while I was in high school but I thought that his story made a lot of sense. So after I got out of the Army I started going to church, taking my family, and sang in the Kingswood Methodist Church choir for ten years. I had a lot of after-hours conferences with the minister discussing philosophical points.

"Attitude is more important than appearance, giftedness or skill. It will make or break a company, a church, a home, a person."

—CHARLES R. SWINDOLL

Eleven

Good People

I BEGAN WRITING LETTERS to businessmen and one of them was Mr. G. A. Campbell of Campbell Industries and Campbell Dairy in Clovis. In my letter to him, I wrote, "Mr. Campbell, I'm a graduate of Clovis High School and I'm spending time in the Army and I don't know you and I don't know about your business except that it's very successful," and so on and so forth and he wrote me back once or twice.

When I returned on leave I went to his office and I asked his secretary if there would be any chance at all of seeing Mr. Campbell. She said, "Let me check." She went in then came back out and said, "He's got about thirty minutes to spend with you, but that's all." I said, "That's okay. I didn't know if I'd get to see him at all." So I went into Mr. Campbell's office, it was about two in the afternoon, and I introduced myself and he said, "What can I do for you? How can I help you?"

"I am a great admirer of the success that you have had and I know that you own the Coca-Cola Bottling Company and your dairy business and ice cream manufacturing and I don't know what else there is."

"Well I also have the Coca-Cola business in Roswell and Tucumcari, New Mexico, and in Albuquerque," he said.

"Wow! How do you manage all those businesses?"

"Well let's just take Campbell's Dairy right here in Clovis. I've got Charlie Murphy. Charlie started working with me right out of high school and now he's about fifty years old and he is a dedicated, loyal manager and I pay him extremely well and leave him alone and he takes care of that business for me."

"That's good advice. How about your Coca-Cola company in Albuquerque?"

"When I got these franchises, nobody wanted them and I got them for almost nothing. I used to drive in a Ford Model T from Clovis to Albuquerque twice a month to help get that business going and it would take me all day since there were no paved roads then. I would drive that Ford Model T in ruts that was supposedly a highway."

So he starts telling me all these stories and goes on and on and finally his secretary stuck her head in the office and said, "Mr. Campbell will there be anything else?" and he said, "Why?"

"Because it's five o'clock and I'm about to go home."

"No there isn't anything else, just lock the front door." And he turns back to me and says, "Now where was I?" We sat there and talked until about six-thirty that evening.

I wrote letters to other people, one was a salesman for McClancy Seasoning Company in Beaumont, Texas. We bought spices from them for the meat packing company. I would write letters and keep files of each letter and I attempted to set up correspondence with important people in that way. It just seemed like a good idea. Having the acquaintance with successful people was instilling in me a desire to one day be a businessman and make a lot of money.

> *A Jewish father was instructing his son about life. He said, "Son, get out there and make a lot of money, and make it honestly if you can."*

I wrote to my wife almost every day and she wrote almost every day until finally she moved to Washington. We got a little apartment in Pasco, Washington. I was stationed out in the middle of nowhere. There was usually somebody on post who had a car, and if we could leave town early enough in the morning and get back to work by check-in time, they wouldn't have a problem with us going home occasionally.

So I would spend four to five nights a week at home in Pasco. The place we had rented was actually a single car garage that had been converted into a little apartment. It had a drop-down Murphy bed and at one end of the garage was the tiniest little kitchen in the world and the tiniest little bathroom in the world. Lunell, having worked for KCLV in Clovis, got a job working for a local radio station.

She got pregnant with our first son, Andy; he was born when I was still in the Army in 1955. She went home to Clovis prior to his birth, and then I took some leave and came home before he was born. I found out that active military people could get a ride on an Air Force transport

Four generations in 1955: my father T. E. Winton, my grandmother Elizabeth (Lizzie) Winton, myself and my first son Andy.

plane. There was a plane that made a courier run, as we called it, and it took off at Moses Lake Air Force Base, Washington, fifty miles from where I was stationed. If I could get over there, I might possibly get a ride on that plane, if they had any room at all.

They had a priority system but they were mainly hauling freight and other things. They had some sling seats in the back of the plane that you could pull down. You could sit on a piece of canvas and lean back and buckle yourself in. It was a rather cold compartment. Of course it was a prop plane but if you could get a ride, it would eventually land in Cannon Air Force Base in Clovis. But first it would go from Moses Lake, Washington, to Hill Air Force Base in Utah, then Tinker Air Force Base in Oklahoma. It was six or seven hours of flying time but would take all day long with all the stops in between.

I found out that people who were on emergency leave would get priority over people who were on regular leave. So working in personnel and being the devious person that I was, I always carried my regular leave papers and also a copy of my emergency leave papers so I would use whichever one was appropriate.

My family would manage to come out to Cannon Air Force Base, seven miles outside of Clovis and pick me up. It was great to be home.

THE UNIVERSAL LAW of cause and effect rules what rewards we will get in life. The effect, or rewards, cannot happen and will not happen without first there being a cause. Service to others is the cause that will determine our rewards, so if we want more, we must first give more.

PART III

Fortitude

My entire life is devoted to setting goals, thinking positive, and doing things bigger and better with the passing of time.

Twelve

Family Style

When I got out of the Army in 1955, I could not find a job. My father and I had developed a few philosophical differences, I guess. I didn't agree with how he was attempting to run his meat packing company and he wouldn't tolerate any interference, so he wouldn't hire me. I went as far as Albuquerque trying all the meat packing operations, but I could not find a job.

So I came back home in the summer and at that time, with the GI Bill, I could get paid $120 a month for going to college and I could rent an old shack in "Vetville" that ENMU had set up near campus. They were old army barracks that had been partitioned into little apartments, but the rent was really cheap. So I went back to college and we moved into Vetville.

Our family grew quickly. Andy was born in May of 1955, Scott was born in October of 1956, Todd was born in March of 1959, and Jeff was born in June of 1961. We had four boys in six years, which was a real handful for Lunell and me, and it put a big financial burden on the two of us.

I also joined the National Guard. At the time, you had to join an active guard unit for three years or be in the Standby Reserves for six years. If you were in the Standby Reserves, they could call you back any time they wanted to. However, if you spent three years in an active guard unit, you'd be discharged once and for all. I took that option, not so much for the three versus six years but for the two days of pay per month I got for being in the Guard.

The captain in charge of our battalion headquarters in Clovis put out the word that he needed someone in the personnel office and so I put myself in for that job.

I came out of the Army as a corporal so I went into the National Guard as a corporal. The Captain said, "Well, uh, do you want to work in here?" And I said, "Yes, I do." Buddy Holmberg was a friend who also had personnel experience. He later owned and operated a jewelry store in Clovis. So the captain decided I would be the personnel sergeant and Buddy would be my assistant. I was then promoted to staff sergeant and I organized the personnel department the same way I had done it in the Army.

After about three or four months I decided that this job called for a sergeant first class (SFC), so I wrote a letter for the captain to sign recommending that I be promoted to SFC. I left it on his desk, and when he returned he saw the letter. Later, when he saw me at the university, he said, "What is this crap about that letter that I found on my desk?"

"Oh, did you find that? Well, I knew that you wanted a well-run personnel department with somebody that's truly responsible and taking charge of it and doing it right and I knew that you'd want to promote me to SFC, so I went ahead and took the initiative and wrote that letter for you."

"You know what? That's a bunch of crap and I'm not the kind of person you can bully around like that. I don't know what you think this is."

I said, "It's up to you."

"What do you mean?"

Family Winton, 1955—Lunell and me with our first-born son Andy.

"Do you want a well-run personnel department or do you want one that will be criticized by everyone that comes along?"

"What are you saying?"

"I'm saying if you want a really well-run department, you will go back and sign that letter."

He did.

I got promoted and even before the first summer camp, I had my own jeep. Our unit was assigned to Fort Sill, Oklahoma, for one summer camp and we went to Fort Bliss on another occasion. Because I had my own private jeep, I would drive out ahead of everybody and park on a hill and watch the convoy go by and then jump back in and pass the guys. I felt like a real big timer.

When I began college the second time, I was scared. I took three three-hour courses that first summer and I was scared to death. I thought that I would be competing with these young kids, the best students, so I got serious about studying for the first time in my life. I thought to myself, "I'm really going to have to dig in and compete because I have to keep this GI money coming in." When I got my grades at the end of the summer for those nine hours, I had an A in all three courses. And I thought, well, I'll be darned.

It only takes a little more effort and the right attitude to go right to the top. One of Earl Nightingale's messages is called "It's Easier to Win." The essence is that ninety-five percent of the population will not do the things it takes to compete and get ahead. That means your only competition is five percent, not everyone else.

Thirteen

What Size, Ma'am?

I HAD THE INCOME from the National Guard, the income from the VA for going to school, but the only job I could find was in Portales, sacking groceries and carrying them out for people. One couple that frequented the store I worked at was Mr. and Mrs. David Turner, and I would always have a little conversation with them when I carried out their groceries. Mr. Turner learned my name. My actual name is Andy Jackson Winton and in the Army everybody had called me Andy, so that lingered. Mr. Turner had retired after twenty-nine years with the J. C. Penney Company and he had come to Portales and opened up a little emporium called Turner's Department Store. Mr. Turner stopped one day and said, "Andy, tell me a little bit about yourself."

"Well," I said, "what would you like to know?"

"When did you get out of the Army?"

"Three or four months ago."

"Do you like working here?"

"Oh, yes. I have a wife and children and so I need to do all I can."

"Well what do they pay you?"

So I told him what it was, maybe seventy-five cents an hour, or a dollar. And he said, "Will you come work for me and I'll give you a raise?"

And I said, "Sure, if you really want me to."

So I worked for him for about two years and actually ran his shoe department. He sent me to Lubbock for the shoe show, to buy the shoes for the department—all those things a department manager does.

That job taught me an awful lot. I found that even if I wasn't an expert on ladies shoes, customer service was what really mattered.

One time a lady came in and said, "I need a pair of party shoes, something special. My husband has this event we have to go to."

So I said, "Well, okay ma'am, do you have anything in mind?"

She said, "Well I want a heel about three inches high and I'd like it to have straps, and some sequins."

So I thought for a moment and said, "I think I've got just what you're looking for." I went back in the stockroom and came out with a pair of shoes.

"My heavens, they're perfect," she said. She tried them on, walked around a little bit and came back and said, "This is exactly what I was looking for."

So I put them back in the box and took the box to the counter and she asked, "Where are you going?"

"I'm going to write an invoice up on these shoes."

"You don't think I'm going to buy the first pair of shoes I try on, do you?"

> *A woman is shopping at the market one day and notices a dirty, drunken, homeless man also shopping. While in line, she dreads to see that he was soon going to be in line behind her and sure enough, he is. He looks at her and looks at her purchases in her basket and says, "Lady, I bet you are single." She wonders how he would know that and scans her items to see what might have given him the clue that*

she truly was single. But she tells him, "Yes I am. How did you know?" He says, "Because you're ugly."

Another time, a lady came rushing into the store just before closing, and she said, "Oh my gosh, I'm in trouble. I have a function that my husband just now told me about and I don't have anything to wear unless I can find the right shoes for the dress I have chosen."

"What do you need?" When she told me, I went to the back and pulled something out. When I came back I said, "How do these look?"

She put them on walked around a little bit, "Oh they're perfect. I'll take them."

So I throw them in the box and hand them to her. She gets ready to go out and says, "Put those on my bill." Mr. Turner had charge accounts for his customers. And she left. That's when I realized even though I'd seen her in the store off and on, I didn't know who she was. So I go upstairs to Mr. Turner's office. He had a little office where he could look out on the store. I said, "Mr. Turner, I really screwed up."

"What happened?"

I told him. "They were $69.95 and you'll have to take that out of my pay. But could you spread that out over about three pay periods?"

And he said, "I'm not going to take it out at all. Don't worry about it."

"No, that's not right. I messed up and it's only fair that I should pay for it. So you take it out of my pay."

"Andy, I'm not going to do that."

"Well what are you going to do?"

"Well we have about 167 charge accounts and I'll just put a $69.95 pair of ladies shoes on every one of them."

"People are going to call down here and complain."

"Right, and everyone who complains I'll take it off."

One day Mr. Turner called me into his office and said, "Ruby and I don't have any children. We've put together a pretty good little fortune and this is a good store and a good business and it's profitable, and if you'll commit to stay here with us, and we've talked this over, we'll leave everything to you."

And I said, "Mr. Turner that is a generous offer, and I can't tell you how much I appreciate it, but this is not what I could be happy doing the rest of my life."

I felt it was too confining to spend all day every day in that one spot in that retail business. I did the best I could do while I was there, but I couldn't see myself doing that for the rest of my life.

Mr. Turner later opened two additional stores, one pretty good sized one in Clovis and one in Tucumcari. I was in the meat packing business by then, but when I knew his store openings were happening, I took off and said, "Mr. Turner, I'm here to report for duty, what do you want me to do to help with this opening?"

He said, "I don't know if I can afford you now."

"You can afford me because I'm working for free."

I worked all day and helped take care of the kids at night. I used to do my homework with Scott lying beside me, holding a bottle in one hand and studying with a book in the other hand. I continued going to college while working at the store. At the beginning of the fall semester, I pretty much did the same thing, I'd jump in there at the front of the class and listen to everything the professor said and take notes. I found that some of the professors were impressed with those of us who were military veterans, so I played that for as much as I could. The next semester I think I made all As again, and by the time I finished school, I was inducted into the Silver Key Society (an academic organization for those who had a certain grade point average).

I enjoyed the business courses. Business was my major: I took business law, economics, insurance and all the other business courses. I remember the business law courses and I remember that I didn't particularly like the accounting courses, but I had to take them.

It is the blessed man who falls in love with his job, because he will never work another day the rest of his life. He will just have fun and enjoyment every day.

Fourteen

Making Bacon

My goal was to be in the meat packing business. Somewhere along the way my father and I reconciled and he asked me to open a new territory and expand our sales of meat products to some eastern New Mexico towns including San Jon, Tucumcari, Santa Rosa and Melrose. It was a run that would be geographically convenient. So I decided that every Tuesday I could take off from everything else and make the rounds, about a 255-mile circuit. Dad agreed to pay me a commission of two percent on everything I sold.

I had saved money in the army and bought a new car. So I would use my car and make this run. I would call on every little greasy spoon restaurant and grocery store and within a few weeks I had built up a pretty good business. Within a couple of months, I was sending out a fully loaded truck with Rancho Packing products for delivery to my customers. I would sell on Tuesday and the meat would be delivered on Thursday and the plant would have Wednesday to put together all the orders to be shipped out.

My father, T. E. Winton, with his grandsons in the early 1960s. (From left) Todd, Scott, Jeff with dad, and Andy.

A railroader, Alton Hare, whose wife worked with my mother, had become a great friend. His nickname was Rabbit. He got a day off every Thursday and he had the job of delivering the meat that I had sold. They called that the "jackrabbit run."

So I'd leave at five-thirty in the morning and I'd be at San Jon, New Mexico, at about seven a.m. when the stores opened. I'd be in Tucumcari about nine or nine-thirty and call on everybody that I could. I would leave there at around noon and I'd make it to Santa Rosa and ultimately back to Melrose near dark. Then I'd come to the meat plant at seven-thirty or eight o'clock that night and leave my order book, and the checks I had collected from last week's business, and any notes that I thought I needed to write. I would then drive back to Portales and get in bed about ten or eleven. I did that week after week after week, in addition to the National Guard, going to college and working at Turner's.

I started calling on people we had never talked to before, and I learned that everything is salesmanship. I found it was easy. Talk to people and

Top photo—
Lunell and me with our four boys, 1962. (From left) Todd, Jeff, Andy and Scott.

Me and my boys, 1962: breakfast together, Christmas morning and ready for Trick-or-Treat.

listen to them. Get to be friends with them. Respect them and the business will come.

I got to know the short order cooks. I was always impressed with how efficient they were at what they did. Most of these little restaurants had a wheel the waitress would clip an order under and the cook would turn it around and read the order and would fill it and he would turn it back the other way and ring a bell when the order was finished and ready to be picked up. He would handle several orders like that at one time. He could be frying eggs and making an omelet and talking to me all at the same time and never miss a beat. I was so impressed by them. While the boys were growing up, I cooked Sunday morning breakfast on a pretty regular basis, and it was usually sausage patties, fried eggs, gravy, and homemade biscuits. I could throw all that together the way Leonard Horner used to do it at the Cozy Corner Café many, many years ago.

I started calling on the butchers at Furr's Supermarkets. My father had not been able to make any inroads with them because these butchers were in their twenties and thirties, but I could relate to them and get along with them. The first time I'd call on them it was just to make their acquaintance and so I said, "I know you're going to tell me that you have all the suppliers you need and you don't need anybody. But I'd just like to get to know you and see if anything works out. So do you mind if I come and see you every once in a while, like once a week for a few minutes?"

So pretty soon I'm asking them things like, "How long have you been with the company? What's your background and experience? Are you married? What's your wife's name? How many children do you have? What are their names?" And so before long it was, "Oh Jack, hi. Come on in, come on in, I'm busy but I have time for you."

I found that getting comfortable with people—listening to them and getting to know about them, being truly and genuinely interested in them, and for them to know that I'm not just blowing smoke—makes them feel important. I really am interested in them. Then when people come to realize that, "He sure makes me feel good, he makes me feel important. What can I do in response?" Subconsciously, they may say, "I can buy what he's selling. That will show my appreciation." Of course, they don't ever spell this out but it's all there psychologically.

I have always told people that, "Selling is not a contest with a winner and a loser. The way you sell people something is by getting on their side of the table and helping them get to where they want to go. With your knowledge and expertise and so on, if people have a need for a home,

Me in my meat packing days.

you can help them. You can help them efficiently and satisfactorily. But it's not like an arm wrestling contest where somebody's going to win and somebody's going to lose. That's not the way selling is done."

Before the summer was over the bank president, Mr. T. E. Willmon, who had loaned some money to my father to finance the meat packing business, wanted to talk to me. I was making a deposit one day and he called me over. He came out of his office and said, "Can I visit with you for a minute?"

"Sure," I said.

I went in and sat down and he said, "What are you doing this summer?"

"I'm working for my dad and helping him build up the meat packing business."

"Well here at the bank we can tell the difference your help has made with the activity of the deposits and so on. What's your plan?"

"Well I plan to work for the summer and then I plan to go back to school." I lacked twelve credit hours to graduate. I had all the required courses but I had to take a music appreciation course and some other

This map shows my stomping grounds when I was running Rancho Packing Company.

little course to actually get a degree. I had all the hard stuff done.

He said, "Well the bank has a loan to your dad on the meat packing company. I know that Edwin Cain has made him a loan too. I was talking to Edwin and we wanted to know if there might be a chance we could buy your dad out of that meat packing company, but keep you to stay and run it."

Mr. Willmon went on, "We'll give you a third of it. I will own a third, Ed Cain will own a third, but you run it." And that's what we did. Mr. Willmon went to talk to my dad and gave him some money, as a form of buying out his business, and suddenly I was in the meat packing business.

When I took Rancho Packing Company over, our sales for that year were approximately $456,000 and we had five or six employees. I was determined to expand the business. There was a grocery store chain headquartered in Hobbs, New Mexico, called Tootie's Cashway. Thomas B. Shnaubert was the owner of it. Anyway I worked my way into being buddies with his butcher. I was there one day when his boss, Kurt Lacass, the supervisor of all the meat markets, was there. We visited and Kurt said, "Do you think that there might be any way that you'd like to service our stores in Lovington and Hobbs and Carlsbad too?" And I said, "Well yeah, if we could, I'd like to look into that."

So to make a long story short, we wound up with a semi truck making that run each week serving Safeway stores and Furr's stores and Cashway stores.

---

*Before you can ever sell your product,
you must first sell yourself.*

Fifteen

High Flying

*Luck is where preparedness
meets opportunity.*

I WAS WORKING LONG HOURS and trying to raise kids. I guess I needed some way to relax, because I didn't have any hobbies. For some reason, I decided I wanted to fly.

Some of my friends helped me get airborne. I don't know why I wanted to fly, but I did. I used to stop in at a bar called the Gold Lantern after work sometimes. There was a regular gang of us there—me, Dr. Elwin E. Crume and Dr. Lynn Abshere. We all agreed that we wanted to fly and knew another guy who might be interested, Andy King, who owned an auto supply store. David Norvell, a lawyer, was also interested. It wasn't such a wild idea. Many people in Clovis knew how to fly because of the long distances they had to travel.

I didn't know if I could afford flying or not. But with my $150 per week salary and a $96 house payment, I was doing better than I had ever done in my life. I joined the flying group in 1962. We all put two hundred dollars into a kitty to raise a thousand dollars and paid it down on a $3,200 Piper Tri-Pacer airplane. I was ready to take off.

> *The definition of flying is hours and hours of sheer boredom punctuated with moments of stark terror.*

> *There is also the Chinese fortune cookie that reads, "Woman who fly upside down, have crack up."*

Of course, I knew I couldn't afford flying lessons, but one day Bud Cagle came to the meat packing company to talk about getting a quarter of beef. He was the partner of two brothers who owned the Ford dealership, Gateway Auto Company. I said, "Bud, somebody told me you are a pilot."

"Yup."

"How long have you been doing this?"

"Oh, forever. That's what I should have made my life's work instead of the car business. I love it."

"Well how much do you know about it?"

"I'm a certified flight instructor."

"No kidding? What would you charge to teach me how to fly this Tri-Pacer?"

"Tell you what, you cut up that nice hind quarter there for my freezer and that will pay me in full."

And I said, "Done. You got a deal."

So Bud and I set about for me to learn to fly. Generally speaking a person will work with their instructor for thirty or forty hours before being allowed to solo. But by the seventh hour that we spent together, he had me doing all kinds of stuff. We would fly the plane, land it, take off and land it again, go out and fly around a section of land. He said, "Next time you come in for a landing, I want you to go over there and pull next to the building."

So I did. And he got out. And I said, "Where are you going? Are you going to get a cup of coffee or something?"

"No. I'm going to watch you fly this airplane by yourself."

I taxied down to the end of the runway and took the plane off thinking, "Man, there's only one way I'm ever going to get back on the ground and that's to land safely." So, I flew around and then landed a couple of times and each time he'd wave at me to go on and do it again. When I landed for my final time, he signed me off for my solo.

For the solo cross country you had to fly to three points and land and then get somebody to certify that you had been at that airport. Another one of the requirements was to pass a written exam. I never failed anything in my life, but I failed that thing two or three times. Finally I had about 250 flying hours logged in my book, but I still was doing it all on a student license. Eventually I passed the thing and had full pilot status for a single engine prop.

I've had a lot of interesting flying experiences through the years, some of which helped me with my business. A customer of mine named Kirk called me one Sunday morning at home and said, "Jack, this is Kirk."

"Kirk, what can I do for you?"

And he said, "I'm in jail."

"Jail?"

"Right. In Hobbs."

He was a good old boy. He'd gone out and partied a little too much, got drunk, was picked up for DWI and got arrested. He said, "Jack, I hate to say this but this isn't the first time this has happened and if my boss finds out about it, I'm fired. I'll be gone and at my age, I never could find another job."

"Well, that's too bad, Kirk…"

"I need you to do something for me."

"What?"

"Come get me out of jail."

"Kirk, how will I get you out of jail?"

"Well I need five hundred dollars bail and I don't have it." The last time this happened, I called my boss and this time you're the only one I can think of who might help me."

So I take five hundred dollars in meat packing money, go out to the airport and get into the little Tri-Pacer and fly to Hobbs and land at the airport. I get a guy to take me to the jail and I get Kirk out.

Obviously Kirk felt indebted to me. So there was one time I said, "Kirk, you know we have been saving hams for Easter." I explained that it was our biggest sales season, so we had raised the price on them somewhat, and if anybody wanted to buy them they could, but it was practically Easter and nobody had committed to any large orders yet. So I was holding some inventory.

He said, "How many do you think you have?"

"Oh probably ten thousand pounds."

And he took a little piece of paper and said, "Okay, send two thousand pounds to store number two and fifteen hundred pounds to store number three and two thousand pounds to store number four and so on. How many is that?"

I said, "Nine thousand."

"Well make it five hundred more for this store and five hundred more for that store."

So we took care of him and he took care of us.

In addition to flying and servicing clients like Kirk, I was working long hours producing meat. On hog killing day (we only killed hogs once a week), I would go to the plant at five-thirty or six in the morning and start heating the water. Then I put some lye and some chemical into the water. Then I would drive in the first five or six pigs into the kill chute, shoot them and "stick them," as they say. I'd hook the hoist to the leg of the first one and pull it up and drop him in the vat of water. Then when the hair started slipping, I would dump him out into the de-hairing machine, which is just sitting there turning the pigs over and over as the hair gets knocked off of them. Then I'd put another one in the water and start the routine again. By the time the employees came to work at seven o'clock, I'd already have five pigs on the floor, one on the table and one in the tank.

For delivery days, we packed and loaded the orders on the truck the evening before. We had to be careful so that the orders were all packed and loaded in the proper sequence for distribution. We put the orders to be unloaded last in the front of the truck and the orders to be unloaded first in the back of the truck. We'd stay there until we had all the orders filled and there were lots of days when I would stay there until ten or eleven o'clock at night. The truck took off at five the next morning to make the first deliveries by seven.

Only we can control what thoughts we allow to enter our mind and to stay there, so we can make those thoughts be whatever we want them to be. We also are the only ones who will dictate how we react to events in our life. That reaction and those thoughts are determined by our attitude.

PART IV

Curiosity

> *It is our duty as men and women to proceed as though limits to our abilities do not exist. We are collaborators in creation."*
>
> —Pierre Teilhard de Chardin

Sixteen

What's Real Estate?

A Realtor named Fred Burch had sold us our home. He was a partner in a company called Bell Real Estate in Clovis. He was a good guy and had given us a square deal. One day I was walking downtown, thinking about my future, when I ran across Fred Burch on the street and he said, "Well, hi Jack. How you doing? How about you come in here and sit down, let's have a cup of coffee."

So we went in a restaurant and he looked across the table and said, "How's it going?" And back in those days, I thought when somebody asked that, they really wanted to know.

So I said, "Well, Fred, it ain't going well."

"What's the matter?"

"Well, let me explain something. When my oldest son was two years old, his mother was shopping in a grocery store, and what with people coming and going she thought he was right beside her, but he had toddled off and followed somebody out of the store. He was a small little guy and he wandered into the road and a car backed over him and broke his leg and his arm. He had tire marks across him. I don't know why it didn't squash him. But at any rate, he was in the hospital in traction for thirty days. And when I got him out of the hospital, they required me to pay a thousand dollars, which I didn't have. I went to one of the banks and was able to borrow the thousand dollars and when it came due in six months, I went across the street to the other bank and borrowed a thousand dollars and put sixty dollars of interest with it and paid the first bank back. And when the second bank's note came due I went back to bank number one and borrowed another thousand dollars and paid the second one back." I said, "That boy is six years old now, and I still owe that thousand dollars."

He looked at me with interest, never saying a word. He finally said, "You know what? You could sell real estate."

"Really? What does a real estate salesman do?"

"Well, you know like when I met you, you meet people. You find out what they need, what they can afford, you familiarize yourself with what's available in town for sale, and you help people get settled into a home."

"My goodness, can you make a living doing that?"

"The top guy in our office last year made over twenty-five thousand dollars."

And here I was thinking I was doing pretty good making $7,800 a year. "Are you kidding me? Is that right?"

We went back to his office, and he gave me a book called *Questions and Answers on Real Estate* by Robert Semenow. He said, "It's easy. All you have to do is learn some stuff and sit down and take a test, and you can get licensed. I'm also going to let you borrow these records." It was an old heavy phonograph album collection that weighed eight or ten pounds, big old records, twelve of them. They were Earl Nightingale's *Lead the Field* program.

He said, "You go home and you study this book and go all the way through it and you also listen to these recordings and then come back and talk to me later."

When I listened to those records, I was amazed. Here was someone who had summed up everything I had been exposed to with regard to work, relationships, religion, success, failure. Mr. Nightingale told me that I am the one who controls my destiny. I am the one who can change my circumstances because I had also created them. He taught that we become what we think about. It was the same message in the Bible in Proverbs: "As a man thinketh in his heart, so is he." The New Testament says, "As ye sow, so shall ye reap." Simple basic stuff, but it finally made sense to me. I don't know, maybe it was my age, but I got the message. To use those tools I had to adopt new habits of thinking and new habits of behavior.

I took the records to a friend of mine named George Tomsco. He was also a member of the Fireballs, a local Clovis band that once had a national hit called "Sugar Shack." They had another big hit called "Bottle of Wine." He was also the best audio genius I knew at the time, so he converted the records to tapes and helped me find a reel-to-reel tape player. I played those tapes every night and fell asleep to them. Maybe it was like subliminal programming, but I started to do the things the tapes said to do.

I sat down every morning and wrote my goals down. I wrote down my purpose, why I was here and I wrote what I wanted to do today, where I wanted to be in five years, ten years. I wrote goals that addressed my family life, my business and my community involvement. I also did what Earl suggested and identified the person I wanted to be. He said to act like that person throughout the day, every day and within thirty days, you would be that person. So I began doing the things that the person I wanted to be would do. I acted as if I was the successful person that I intended to be. And I started to become that person.

About a month or two after I had last met with Fred, I came down to his office and said, "Well I'm here to talk to you. What do I do now?"

He said, "Have you read the book?"

"Yeah."

"Do you think you know the answers?"

"I hope."

"Well, you have to go to Albuquerque and take the state test. I'll fill out an application for you."

So I went up there—actually I flew the old Tri-Pacer airplane up there. Two ladies that were also going to take the test had driven up there and they agreed to come pick me up at the airport. We went to dinner and talked real estate until ten o'clock or so and got up the next morning and went to take our tests. We took our exam and were told that the results would be mailed to us later. I knew that even if I didn't pass the exam, I was going to make some sort of change.

We had a sharp young fellow who had joined our meat packing company named Moreland Martin. Moreland was a very impressive guy. In fact at one point he had cut meat on a television show in New York City. He wore a tuxedo and they billed him as the nation's leading expert on meat cutting techniques. We were lucky to get him. He was originally from our area and that was the only reason we got him.

He was a guy with a big ego, like a lot of us. He and I got to be good buddies and our wives got along well with each other. We stayed friends for a long time.

I made him a manager. He had been working in the management position for a couple of months and was calling a lot of shots and I told him, "Moreland, I'm thinking seriously of turning this business over to you to run." And he agreed.

About two weeks later, Fred called me at the meat packing business one Saturday morning. "Jack, you've passed the test and I have your license here," he said. "What are you going to do?"

And I said, "Golly bum, Fred, I don't know."

"Well, you can start selling real estate if you want to. We'll do a little training for you."

"Okay, when's your sales meeting?"

"Monday morning at nine."

I said, "I'll be there."

So I told Moreland the time had come.

I called Mr. Willmon at the bank to let him know about my plans and to help him get acquainted with Moreland.

As it turns out, the meat packing business was in the process of changing. It's a very competitive business. Swift & Company is lucky to have a profit of two percent from sales. We were continuously under pressure. There was more and more pressure for USDA inspection, and with our old worn-out building and equipment, we would never have passed.

So we subsequently closed the plant. Moreland wound it down and closed it and he became a real estate salesman too. He sold farms and ranches and was very successful. He had been raised in Fort Sumner, New Mexico, in an agricultural family, so he knew the industry.

The last year that I ran that meat packing business we had sales of about $4.5 million and twenty-five employees. It had grown quite a bit. Although we were expanding, we weren't making much money. I was taking home a salary of only $150 a week. My partners would have allowed me to pay myself more if I had wanted to, but the business wasn't profitable like it should have been. We were lucky if we made fifty thousand dollars a year on $4.5 million in sales because there was just so much overhead.

I was tired of the work and the long hours. I decided, kind of like at Mr. Turner's store, that I didn't want to pack meat for the rest of my life. After seven years, it was time for some other kind of work and with just having passed the real estate exam, real estate is what it would be.

"To prospect for your own acres of diamonds, develop a skill we might call 'intelligent objectivity'— the skill to stand back and look at your work as a person from another planet might look at it. With that objectivity we can look within the framework of our industry or profession and objectively ask ourselves: Do you know all you can know about your industry or profession? How can the customer be given better service?"

—Earl Nightingale

Seventeen

Selling Property Door-to-Door

WHEN I FIRST STARTED OUT selling real estate, I was working strictly on commissions, and I was stretched pretty thin. Not only was it a challenge to make my first sale, but it took three months to get loans approved and for me to get paid.

I became very good friends with a lady on the telephone at the Veterans Administration. I had a direct VA home loan for our personal home with no lender in between. And she would call me on the phone and say, "Mr. Winton, when are you going to be able to make this payment?"

And I would say. "I am not sure, but believe me I will pay it."

"I don't know how long I can hold tight here and sit on it."

"Well, just do the best you can for me, please."

I would tell her everything, "I'm in a new business where I think I can make money and I have sold three homes in the last two weeks that are going to close the fifteenth of next month and so on…and then I think I'll be able to catch up on the payments."

And she'd say, "Okay, but I'm really catching a lot of heat over this. You're three months behind now."

"Yes ma'am, I understand that."

There was a grocery store called JO's Food Market where we set up a charge account. But JO's Food had to cut me off after three months. "I can't carry you any longer," the owner said. "I know your wife comes in and buys groceries but I just can't do this any longer." My wife was working but not in something that produced income. She was raising four children and managing a household.

I was scared to death about my first sale. I didn't know what to do or where to start, so my broker gave me a little book and said to study these listings and learn them. It gave the address and details about all the homes listed for sale.

So I memorized them and drove around all over town looking at the houses and then I said, "Now what?" And the people in the office said, "Well, pick you out a place and make yourself the expert of the area. Treat it like your farm and become the expert for the area you pick."

I picked out an area of town, not the best area, and I went down the street knocking on doors. I would say to whoever answered, "Hi, I'm Jack Winton, here is my card, do you want to buy any real estate? No? Do you want to sell any real estate? No? Do you know anybody who does? No? If you come across anybody who has an interest in buying or selling real estate, would you maybe tell them that I was by and met you, unless you've got somebody else you refer business to?"

So I was doing that during the first week of being in business. I knocked on a door at 416 Rencher Street as I recall. And the biggest guy you ever saw came to the door and he said, "What do you want?"

And I said, "My name is Jack Winton, I'm in the real estate business, here is my card. Do you want to buy any real estate?"

"No I don't."

"Do you want to sell any real estate?"

"No I don't."

"Do you know anybody who does?"

"I don't think so, just a minute." He turned around and said, "Hey Kaywood, you wanna buy a house?"

"I don't know. I might."

So a couple named Alec and Elizabeth Kaywood came out. They were a military family with Cannon AFB. And it turns out that the big guy was already stationed at Cannon and Alec and Elizabeth had just arrived for an assignment. So I made an appointment to go out with them. I showed them houses and before the end of the week I signed them up on a contract. That was my first sale. It was a forty thousand dollar sale and real estate commissions were five percent, so it created about two thousand dollars of commission. The salesman split back then was never better than fifty-fifty, so there was a thousand dollars that came to me at the closing.

Not too long after that, Dean Eldridge, who was the broker in the company, came by my little half desk—he had an office in the corner of the building, but the sales people had little half desks—and he said, "How you doing, Jack?"

"Pretty good."

"Anything I could help you with?"

"Well, I'm supposed to have an appointment with Delmon Farris and his wife tonight and I'm nervous and scared about it." Delmon had recently returned from the Marines where he had been an officer. Great big tough guy with a crew cut. He had recently taken a job as the principal of an elementary school.

"Well what time's your appointment?"

"Six-thirty this evening."

"Would you like me to go with you?"

"I'd love for you to go with me."

So we go and old Dean sits down and he begins. "How's your new job working out? How did you like the Marines? What made you decide to quit?" He visited and visited and visited with them and said, "I know you've already looked at some houses with Jack because we talked about this together. Sounds to me that, based on the school that you're the principal of, that certain address is the right one for you. What do you think?"

And Delmon said, "Well, we like that one pretty good."

"Then let's just do some 'what ifs' here."

So he whips out a contract and he said, "How would you take title? Delmon C. Ferris and Angela E. Ferris, man and wife." And he had the listing printout, so he wrote, "Lot 6, Block 13." Pretty soon he had the whole contract filled out and he said, "Did you notice that I put in here that you are offering two thousand dollars less than their asking price? This is a good deal already, so if we can get this done for you, you're going to be way ahead in this situation."

And all the time Dean is getting my buyer to say "Okay, Okay, Okay." So he turned around and held the pen out. And he held it there, and they looked at him, and he didn't bat an eye and pretty soon my buyer reached up there and took the pen and signed the contract and handed it to his wife. She signed it. We thanked them for the business and got in the car and drove.

Once in the car, I said, "That was the most masterful job I have ever seen in my entire life."

"Well, you made a nice sale," Dean said. "I didn't do a damn thing. You did it all."

That guy taught me more than anybody ever did.

After he taught me to do that, I used the technique frequently. I am not forcing anyone. I just ask myself: "Is it the right thing for them?" And then I say, "Let me just try something here." They're sitting at the desk and I whip out a contract and say, "How would you take title to the property, first name, second name…" I can see out of my peripheral vision that they are whispering to each other but I just keep on writing. And he's turning to her and saying, "What's he doing?"

"Looks to me like he's writing a contract."

"Are we ready to do this?"

"I don't know."

So I just keep writing the contract and then I say, "Let me read this back to you and see if it sounds right. This is your name, right?"

"Yeah."

"This is the property we're talking about, address and so on."

"Right."

"I tell you what, the right price to offer might not get it done but this is the right price…" and I continue through the contract. "So far so good. Does that sound all right?"

"So far so good."

"Well let's just give it a try." And I stick the pen out there. And at that point the one who speaks first is the one who buys it. You're just helping them to do what they need to do.

> *A traveling salesman on a country road had a flat tire and no jack. He saw a farm house up on a hill and thought, "I will go borrow a jack from that farmer." As he was walking, he started thinking to himself, "I bet that farmer is in the field still working. He will be upset with me for interrupting his work and will not loan me his jack." He kept walking and realized the sun was going down. He thought to himself that the farmer was probably now putting up his tools and will be busy and will not loan out his jack. He kept going and saw a light come on in the house. He thought to himself that the farmer is probably sitting down to dinner and will be upset for the interruption and will not loan me his jack. He then saw the light go off and thought "Oh no, now the farmer has gone to bed and he will be very upset with me and will not loan me his jack."*
>
> *The salesman finally got to the front porch, knocked on the door, the farmer opened the door and the salesman said, "Just keep your damn jack."*

Another technique I used one time: I had some pretty hard customers who were trying real hard to buy a house but were offering a really low price that I didn't think would work. When I wrote up the contract, I wrote in the remarks section that this agreement is to include all the furniture in the living room, including the sofa and lamps, etc.

I showed them the contract and they said, "What's this? We don't want their damned furniture."

And I said, "Well, I'm trying to find a point to negotiate so work with me here. You're offering a really low price and I don't even know if they are going to consider it. But we'll see if we can make a little distraction here by talking about the furniture."

So they said, "Okay, you know your business."

So I took the contract to the listing agent and we presented it to the seller. Reading it over, the seller said, "Furniture in the living room including the sofa and everything? Well that's the most ridiculous thing I've ever seen. We're not going to do that."

"Look, just mark it out and initial it and we'll just say that you would not even consider that."

"Yeah, well all right." And he marked it out and initialed it and I said, "Well I don't know. Let me find out if they are going to stand still for this."

I took the contract back to the buyers and said, "You bought the home."

They said, "What about the furniture?"

"He said he wouldn't even consider selling you the furniture."

They said, "We didn't want it anyway."

Do not argue with an idiot. He will drag you down to his level and beat you with experience.

Following the dictates of Earl Nightingale, I set goals. In late fall of 1963 I said, "If Dean Eldridge could make twenty-five thousand dollars selling real estate I don't know why I can't." So I took a spiral notebook like Earl Nightingale suggested and wrote the date at the

Selling Property Door-to-Door / 103

I learned about setting goals and did what Earl Nightingale suggested—I wrote my goals daily. These notebooks represent about five years worth of daily goals.

top and wrote my 1964 goal: "I will earn twenty-five thousand dollars selling real estate in 1964. The following ideas and thoughts will help me reach this goal."

So I would sit down for twenty-five or thirty minutes every day and write down suggestions that I felt would be beneficial to make that happen. I did not make twenty-five thousand dollars that year but I earned $18,700, two and a half times what I had ever earned as a butcher. At the end of that year, I said, "I think I'm onto something here."

So the next year I sat down and wrote a goal: "I will earn fifty thousand dollars in 1965 selling real estate, and the following ideas will help me to reach this goal." I didn't earn fifty thousand dollars, but I made thirty-six thousand dollars that year and along the way began selling for Town & Country Real Estate, the startup of Dean Eldridge and Bob Burch. It was located in Clovis across from the hospital on Thornton Street. That's where I made my first big deal, which fell right into my lap.

A guy walked in the office one day. I was the only one there and I said, "Can I help you sir?"

"Yeah," he said. "I want to sell a piece of land."

"Where is it?"

"Out by House, New Mexico." House was a very small farming community out in the middle of nowhere.

He said, "I'm not sure where it is because I'm from Phoenix, Arizona. It belonged to an aunt and uncle and I've just been notified that I inherited it. But I'm here to sell it and I want to get it done."

"Well let's you and I go down to the ASC office, the local soil conservation office."

There was a fellow that I had met named Ivey who worked there. So we went and I said, "Ivey, this gentleman has a legal description for a piece of land and he doesn't know a thing about it. What can you tell us?"

So he goes and opens up some books and comes back to us and says, "Well here's an aerial photo of the area. I understand that this has a pretty good wheat crop on it. I'm not sure but this year is a pretty good year for wheat."

So my seller asked, "Well what do you think the land is worth?"

"Oh gee, I don't know," Ivey said. "It depends on how long someone wants to have it on the market for sale. Sometimes you can price something and if you expose it to the market, you might find a buyer, but that's sort of a hit or miss thing."

So I said to the guy, "Do you want me to list the property for you and see if I can sell it?"

And he said, "I just want to sell it." It was 160 acres.

"What will you take for it?"

"If I can get a hundred thousand dollars, I'll take it and walk off."

"It might be worth more than that, especially with a wheat crop on it," I said.

"I just want to get it sold."

I asked, "Can you stay in town overnight?"

"Yeah."

"Good. Come back to see me tomorrow morning."

So I go to my brother-in-law, Howard Cox, my sister Bette's husband, and I said, "Howard, I think we may have an opportunity here. Let's get in the car and drive out there and take a look at this land." We did and it had a beautiful wheat crop on it. It was dryland wheat that looked like it was going to make twenty to thirty bushels to the acre. Wheat was going for $2.50 a bushel and I said, "The guy says he will take a hundred thousand dollars for it."

Howard said, "Let's buy it."

I said, "Where are we going to get a hundred thousand dollars?"

And he said, "Well I think I can get it. I've got some connections at the bank. Howard Martin at the Clovis National Bank goes to church with me."

Within twenty or thirty minutes we found we could get the money and close on the land. We bought that piece of land, had the wheat crop harvested and Howard cut me in on the deal—he had all the money in it. I did make more than just a real estate commission and Howard made out like a bandit, but the man who sold it called the shots, so what can I say?

"*Our rewards in life will always match our service.*" It's another way of saying, "As ye sow, so shall ye reap." It's been written in many ways, in every language on earth. It is the universal law of cause and effect. If we want more rewards, we must first increase our service.

Eighteen

Can't Say No

Some guys in the office were studying for the broker exam. I had only been there a few months when they said, "Jack, why don't you meet with us to prepare and study for this broker test that's coming up?"

"I don't know if I want a broker's license."

"Well you don't have to be a broker, you can get the license and still do what you do now."

I said, "Okay."

I wanted to become buddies with some of these people that I worked with so we started studying for this brokerage test. Three of us drove together to Albuquerque to take the brokerage exam and when we got the word back, I was the only one who passed the test.

> *There was this golfer. He loved golf and played it all the time. He came home one Saturday and his wife said, "How was your golf game?"*
>
> *He said, "I'm quitting. I'm not going back."*
>
> *"What do you mean? Why not?"*

Well my eyesight's gotten so bad. I can never see where the ball goes."

"Why don't you take my brother?" she said. "His eyesight is really good."

And the golfer said, "Come on, he's ninety-three years old, I'm eighty-five."

"Well go and try it anyway."

So the next day he goes out on the golf course and brings the brother-in-law on the cart. He gets out and he hits the ball down the fairway and he turns to the brother-in-law, "You see where the ball went?"

And he said, "Yep, sure did."

The golfer said, "Where'd it go?"

The brother-in-law said, "I can't remember."

The state of New Mexico used to put a little notice in the papers announcing who passed the broker exam and where they were from. So there was a little notice in the paper that I had passed the exam and one day an old real estate investor, a wealthy man named M. C. Roberts, came by the office. He had a funny way of talking and he came to see me and said, "Have ya found a place for your real estate office yet? I read in the paper that you got a broker's license."

"Yes sir that's true."

"Well, you're gonna go in the real estate business aren't you?"

I said, "No."

"I don't know why not."

"Well, for one thing, I don't have the money and you can't do that on nothing, you know?"

So he said, "Come get in my car."

He took me to a beautiful office building that was nearing completion, and it was divided into three suites of about one thousand to eleven hundred square feet each. When he took me into the least completed one, he said, "I'll let you pick the paneling that goes on the walls and the carpet on the floor and anything else not already installed." It had two bathrooms, including a private bathroom for the principal office. And he said, "And I'll give you six months of rent free while you get your feet on the ground. Now you think about that."

> *They say that everyone buys real estate. Some buy it for themselves, others buy it for their landlord.*

A few days later I went to my brother-in-law, Howard, who's in the grocery business. I guess I was killing time, sitting there, and he was sitting at his desk and he said, "What's the newest thing in the real estate business?"

"Well, Mr. Roberts is bugging me about opening a real estate office because now I have a broker license."

"Well why don't you?"

I said, "Howard, I don't have the money to do that."

"How much money do you have?"

"I've checked around. I have a life insurance policy and if I borrowed the cash value, I could get $2,300."

"How much would you need to open an office?"

"At least five thousand dollars. That would be to make a down payment on some office equipment and pay the utility deposits and hire somebody."

So he sat there for a minute, opened his desk drawer, wrote out a check, flipped it to me and said, "Okay, there's another $2,700. Now you've got five thousand dollars. So you're either gonna have to think of another excuse or go do it."

I took his $2,700 and put in the paperwork to get my $2,300 from the insurance company and began negotiation with an office supply store. It was an old family-owned business called Goodman Office Supply. Johnny Mack Goodman said, "Take me up and show me the facility." So I did and he said, "Let me take care of everything."

"What do you mean?"

He came back with a list and said, "This is the secretarial desk, this is the settee, this is the coffee table, this is the lamp that goes in the corner, this will be your desk and chairs back here. We've got these four little offices back here."

I said, "How much is this gonna cost?"

"That's not the important thing." Of course, he made money on it. "The important thing is could you handle a down payment of a thousand dollars and monthly payments of $268 a month?"

"I probably could."

So he set the whole thing up. And there I was in the real estate business before I knew it. I opened my real estate company in 1965, and I gave it a really original name: Jack Winton Realty.

EARL NIGHTINGALE said that when you practice the principles in the Lead the Field *program, the things you need to fulfill your goals begin to come to you when you need them. This is the law of attraction. It happens with or without goals, because we get what we think about, whether it's through disciplined thinking or not. Like the person going through life saying they need to lose weight. The universe will keep them in a state of needing to lose weight until they change their self-talk.*

Nineteen

Building the Business

My first employee was a secretary named Gail Zydell. My second was a sharp fellow named Denton Lambert, a college graduate, and he was the Morton's potato chip route man—so I had been bumping heads with him for years when I had been selling meat to stores. When I opened my real estate company, he came to see me. He said, "Tell me honestly how have you done in real estate selling?"

I said, "Well I was over at Town and Country Real Estate and I did very well, I made twice as much as I ever would have in the meat business."

"How do you think I would do?"

"I think you would do as well or even better. You're a personable, happy, enthusiastic young fellow."

"Okay I'm going to quit Morton's and work for you."

Lonny Allsup had sold his Lonny's convenience stores in Roswell to Southland Corporation and he had a non-compete clause within the same geographic area, so he came to Clovis. He came to the real estate office that I was working in and he introduced himself and said, "I want to get back into business. I have quite a bit of capital from my sale to the Southland Corporation so I want to buy some grocery stores that would be appropriate for my kind of business."

I knew everybody in the grocery business so I said, "Okay, I can help you." I sold Lonny three stores. In fact it turned out that after Lunell and I had bought a new home, he and his wife Barbara bought one two doors up from us. One of the guys who had sold his store to Lonny, Charlie Bell, said, "Well I don't have anything to do now, so how about I come and sell real estate with you, Jack?" I said, "Come ahead."

Soon I had a pretty good little group of sales people.

Then I started a movement to begin a multiple listing service in Clovis. There had never been one. All there had been was the most disorganized bunch of Realtors ever. They would have hip pocket listings and really did not serve the public adequately. So I got some of the guys to come together for a breakfast meeting and said, "Let's have a real multiple listing service. It's worked in other places, so why not here?" Roswell had a very active MLS community so we went there and talked to them. Soon we started the multiple listing service in Clovis.

I became acquainted with a lady whose husband had been a doctor in town, but he had passed away from multiple sclerosis. She was very well educated and upon his death, she decided she was going to go teach school. So she went to teach school and after a year she decided she didn't like that worth a darn. So she quit and started selling real estate for one of my competitors and she was cracker-jack good at it. She had an opportunity to sell one of my listings through the multiple listing service so she and I had the opportunity to go make the presentation and ink (or close) the sale.

It was only a short while until I had the opportunity to sell one of her listings and not long after that she came and said, "I want to work for you. I want to change my license."

Marie Dandrea was her name. She practically made my business. She

Me in 1970 when I had Jack Winton Realty.

was probably fifty years old or so, had completely gray hair, was short and stocky, but was a frisky thing. The other sales reps really didn't like her very much because when she would hear other agents talking, she would somehow end up with their prospect. She would solicit her own prospects plus she would try to work with other agents' customers. But she got the job done.

One time, she took a vacation and went to Italy where her husband was from. She must have been having a great time because after she'd been gone about a month, she called me on the phone and said, "Jack,

I'm gonna stay a little longer. I want you to put five thousand dollars into my account at the Citizen's bank." Click, she hung up.

I didn't know where she was, or where she called from so I didn't have the chance to tell her I didn't have the money and wasn't able to do this. I went down to my banker friend Mr. Willmon and I said, "Do you know Marie Dandrea," and he said, "Oh yeah."

"Well listen to this story: she just called me from somewhere in Italy, said she was having a good time and wasn't gonna be coming home for a week or two and said to deposit five thousand dollars into her account here."

"Well what are you going to do?"

"Well, I don't know, I don't have the money. What would you do?"

"I'd put five thousand dollars into Marie Dandrea's account."

"And what if I'm short?"

"You sign a note for it."

Well I did, and that cemented our friendship and she was loyal, faithful and true and continued to "rob" from other sales agents. The multiple listing reported all the sales that were made, and Marie became the number one sales person of the year for three years running and was making herself and our company a lot of money. She was earning herself fifty to sixty thousand dollars a year and back in those days, with a fifty-fifty split between the company and the agent, my company was earning the same amount.

> *You do not need a parachute to skydive. You only need a parachute to skydive more than one time.*

I wound up with more females than males working for me at Jack Winton Realty, and I enjoyed it. After a couple of years I moved into a bigger building and ultimately had about seventeen sales reps and most of them were females. There was a month in which sixty-five percent of all the sales made in town were from my office.

And then the multiple listing group decided that it was no longer appropriate to reveal who made what sales. They got tired of looking at our numbers.

I didn't sell very much on my own because I spent most of my time managing. I learned from experience that giving jobs to the right people and then leaving them alone to do their job is the way to go.

I began teaching people how to take the real estate test and pass it. I would run an ad in the paper, "Opening a class for aspiring real estate people. Call for reservations, maximum twenty people," and then I would meet with them on Wednesday evening for eight straight weeks, and I'd charge them thirty dollars because if people don't pay for something, they don't value it. And in that period of time I'd get a chance to study and become acquainted with all these people and I would decide which one, or two, or three of them I would want to hire after they got their license. So that's how I filled out my office with sales reps.

We cannot change the past, we cannot change the fact that people will act in a certain way. We cannot change the inevitable. The only thing we can do is play on the one string we have, and that is our attitude. I am convinced that life is ten percent of what happens to me and ninety percent of how I react to it. And so it is with all of us.

Twenty

Meeting the Master

We'd have our weekly sales meeting on Monday morning about nine o'clock in a room with a long conference table that everyone would sit around.

"The first thing we're going to do is to turn off the lights and listen to a twenty minute Earl Nightingale message. The reason we're going to turn off the lights is because I don't want somebody looking across at the wart on somebody's nose and being distracted. I want you to concentrate on this message and don't think about anything else except what you're hearing, because this message will take you wherever you want to go in life. So lights off, punch the button, listen to the message." At the end of it, "Lights back on, now let's talk about business." We would go around the table, and each agent would tell everybody what listings they took the previous week, what contracts they wrote the previous week and any learning experiences they had that everybody else could benefit from.

I had a salesman named Don Rury, who was quite a character. I continuously taught the sales people to find something likeable about every customer. However long it takes, however hard you have to look, you have to find something you like, and once you do, you tell them you've noticed this or that about them and that you appreciate it so much because it marks them as an outstanding person.

In one of the sales meetings, Don Rury said, "Well, I had a real problem with a client this week. I tried my best to find something to like about her, something that I could compliment. But she was fat and ugly and noisy and loud, boxing her four children around the ears all the time I was trying to show houses to them, and I thought I was going to lose it. However, I finally came up with something, so I said, 'You know, ma'am. You sweat less than any fat lady I ever knew.'"

At one point I read an advertisement from Earl Nightingale that he was looking for people to distribute his training materials. So I made a phone call and talked to a guy named Danny O'Neil. He was at one time a major singer, a tenor. I discussed the opportunity of distributing their material to people in New Mexico. So I traveled to Chicago and met with Danny and Lloyd Conant and Earl Nightingale. I spent several days there and made a deal to become their distributor for the state of New Mexico. I wrote them a check for twenty-five thousand dollars worth of product. They had me travel back to Chicago once or twice to speak to audiences about the benefits of the Earl Nightingale program and what it had done for me.

On one visit, I thought I was scheduled to speak the next day, but when I got off the plane in Chicago, the people said, "Hurry, hurry, hurry, we've got to get you to the meeting that's going on."

"What's the big rush, I'm still working on my speech for tomorrow."

They said, "No, no, no, your speech is today."

"What about my luggage?"

"Don't worry, we'll get somebody to bring your luggage."

So they threw me in a car and rushed me to the auditorium. There were about five hundred people sitting there and I didn't know anything about them, other than they were prospective distributors of the

Earl Nightingale products. They marched me down through the middle of this crowd up onto the stage and they put a string around my neck with a microphone and said, "You're on."

So I said, "This is a big surprise. I'm first of all going to say that out in our part of the country they say everyone is a lover or a fighter or a wild horse rider. I have never tried riding wild horses but I know that's what I am."

I only had a general idea of what I wanted to talk about but not specific topics. I had to just wing it and sometimes that's the best thing to do, I guess. I decided to speak to them honestly and sincerely and I said, "I have become aware of what this philosophy, what ingraining this way of thinking into your mind can do for you, and I am so sorry, for example, that my father never had an opportunity to know of the Earl Nightingale philosophy. He worked harder than anybody I ever knew, was more diligent, dedicated and he tried everything, one thing after another after another after another, and never had any major success at any of them. And he passed away at an early age thinking of himself as a complete failure in life.

"And if he had had the opportunity to be exposed to the Earl Nightingale messages and had a grasp of these principles, there's no telling what he could have done. It would have been a whole different story of his life. And that's why I feel that we, all of us in this room, have an opportunity to serve people in a way that is unbelievable."

I finished my little speech, which was emotional at the end, and said, "Thank you. You've been a wonderful audience." And I stood there.

Nothing happened. I took the microphone off and called a fellow over and handed it to him. As I started to step down off the stage, the most tumultuous roar occurred—everybody stood and applauded and it just went on and on.

That night, at a banquet held with these people, I noticed that they had a place at the table for me next to Earl Nightingale. He turned to me and said, "From what I hear of this afternoon, maybe I ought to

Earl Nightingale

start thinking about retiring. Maybe you're gonna take over!" He was just kidding of course. He turned out to be a warm, happy, wonderful person throughout the evening. This was a special evening and I realized how lucky I was to be there.

I really am pleased that I had the opportunity to know Earl Nightingale. It's not as if we were intimate friends, but he called me by name. I even arranged for him to come to our area and give the primary address for the graduating class of Texas Tech University. I had proposed to the Nightingale organization that they get in touch with Texas Tech and offer Earl as a speaker. I told them that while he was there, it would be a big benefit to me in helping to distribute the Nightingale material, so he was happy to do it. Of course, we all went over to Lubbock and had a special reserved seat and listened to him give his talk. And basically he said, in person, the same thing that he says in his messages.

I opened an office in order to distribute his product in Albuquerque and I hired some people but it never really got off the ground. It was just one of the things that I have tried in life that didn't work. Not everything has. But I spent quite a bit of time there at the office in Albuquerque with people that I had recruited. I used to take them out to dinner, and entertain them, and work with them, but it never did take off.

It didn't diminish in any way the value of that philosophy to me, and I have distributed it to some extent ever since. Earl Nightingale re-recorded the program at a later time in life but his voice had lost some of the mellowness and some of the convincing qualities that he had had earlier. I happened to have an opportunity two years ago to get one of the original copies of his messages.

I often loan it and tell them what it could do for them. I tell them, "Any time you're driving today, put that CD in your car and listen to it. If you will listen, and open your mind to this message, this philosophy and way of thinking, it can take you wherever you want to go." Some people do, and some don't. But that's nature.

In fact, Earl Nightingale said, "You start one hundred young men out in life giving all of them exactly the same opportunities. When they reach sixty-five years of age, five of them will be independently wealthy. Fifteen of the one hundred will be well fixed financially, but not wealthy. Sixty-seven of them, though, will be flat broke and have to live on Social Security." And he said, "There's about five percent of the people who will hear the message and live life to their full potential. It's such a small number who will internalize it and use it, the rest of them don't."

You can become anything that you want to become in life and you will become what you think about. You can control your thoughts. Nobody can force you to think certain things. You and only you can determine what is put into your mind and what is kept in your mind. So, it's up to you. It's up to every individual to make of themselves whatever they can, because they will gravitate in the direction of their thoughts and the universe will bring them things that reflect those thoughts.

I even introduced my girls to Earl Nightingale. According to Joy, my second wife, "Every day at breakfast, Jack would take the tape player out and he would punch the button and every morning we had a different Earl Nightingale message to listen to. The girls grew up with that on their breakfast table and that was a big influence on them."

I also had my sons listen to the tapes every morning at breakfast. Some tell me they still listen to them.

I BARGAINED *with life for a penny,*
And life would pay no more.
However, I wept at evening
When I counted my scanty store.
But life is a just employer.
She pays you what you ask.
But once you've set the wages,
Then you must bear the task.
I worked for a menial's hire,
Only to learn dismayed,
That whatever price I had asked of life,
Life would have willingly paid.

Twenty-one

RTPSF/RWF

In my real estate office everyone was listening to Earl Nightingale and writing down their goals and I was preaching constantly that we should "Give people service, don't worry about the rewards; treat them nice, treat them well, but give them service. The rewards will take care of themselves." In fact we had a sign over the door going out of the office:

RTPSF/RWF.

I asked my agents, "Do you know what that means?"

"No."

"Remember To Put Service First / Rewards Will Follow. And every time you walk out that door with a client or to go meet one, you look up at that sign and read what it says and then remember when you get there. You're there to give them service, good service, because everything else will fall into place by itself."

So that's what we did. And it worked.

In the 1960s and 1970s when our small town of Clovis had a population of over twenty thousand people, our company, Jack Winton Realty, Inc., would have over one hundred listings at any given time. It wasn't unusual for us to have as many as fifty sales in a month. We were doing really well.

Shortly after I had opened Jack Winton Realty, Denton Lambert, who first joined me as a salesperson, approached me with an interest in homebuilding, and wanted to start a homebuilding company. So we formed a company called Lambert & Winton, Inc. At one point, our company was building as many as three hundred homes a year. They were entry-level homes that were part of an FHA program. Because the homes met the standards of the program, they were quite inexpensive—the lowest priced new homes available. We built in Clovis and Albuquerque and Portales and other small towns. This was about 1965 or so. Denton worked with me and had an office in my real estate business and ran the building business from there.

Then we purchased a company from Paul Garrison that did electrical, plumbing, and heating and cooling. His company was named Paul Garrison Plumbing Company, but we changed it to L&W Service Company, another really un-original name. Paul had two sons who were not interested in running a viable business. So we bought his business for nearly nothing and kept him on. He was a jewel. He was a fine old man, about seventy years of age, but he could turn out more work than anybody and he knew everyone in town—every supplier and everything important. We did the electrical, plumbing, and heating and cooling work on our houses of course, but we also did work for other homebuilders and the general public. It was a somewhat profitable business.

> *The plumber finished the job and handed the lady of the house his bill. She looked at it, blinked, and said, "My husband is a brain surgeon and he doesn't charge this much." The plumber said, "When I was practicing brain surgery, I didn't either."*

I continued focusing on the real estate business and gave very little time to L&W Service. Denton ran that. He was a brilliant guy and had a mind like a steel trap! He had a degree in accounting from Texas Tech University, where he had had a football scholarship. Denton was a big old guy, but just a teddy bear and a wonderful person. He ran that business during the years that we were buying lots for a thousand to twenty-five hundred dollars and selling an eleven hundred square foot home for ten thousand dollars. Denton was a genius at finding ways to cut costs.

There was one year, 1970, that L&W Service made a good deal of money and so Denton and I decided that each of us would drive a brand new Cadillac. We bought the biggest, finest models they had. Mine was light brown and his was green. We spent money on other things as well. Our accountant met with us and said, "If you'd like to make any charitable contributions this is a good year to do that. We can write it off."

So Denton said, "Well I'd like to help with the educational building they are completing at my church, the Central Baptist Church." My church, Kingswood Methodist, wanted to buy a new pipe organ that cost about ten thousand dollars so I said, "Denton, why don't we make a contribution of ten thousand dollars to the Central Baptist Church for the educational building and ten thousand dollars to the Kingswood Methodist Church to buy a new pipe organ." And so we did.

> *Going to church doesn't make you a Christian any more than standing in a garage makes you a car.*

As our business became more successful through the years, Denton's wife became more self important and for some reason felt justified in giving Denton and me orders on how things were going to be. We usually just ignored her. In 1972, however, she decided to take it to another level, I guess, and walked into my office one day and made some demands that I thought were unreasonable. So I turned around and picked up the phone from my credenza and called L&W Service and said, "Let me speak to Denton."

Denton came on the phone and I said, "Denton, your wife is here and is making some demands that I have absolutely no intention of accepting, so I need to meet with you this afternoon and decide whether you are going to buy my part of the business, or if I'm gonna buy your part of the business, and I hope your wife is out of my office by the time I get off the phone." And I hung up the phone. Then I got up and started around the desk and she left quickly.

To settle this, Denton and I met within the next few days with our accountant Jeff Jacobs and a tax attorney Jim Hart. I said, "Look, Denton, you know more about this business than I do. But that's neither here nor there. Let's do what the two little boys did when they had only one apple between them. One of the little boys said, "You cut it in half and I'll take first choice." So let's agree to let one or the other of us name a price and the other can buy at that price or sell at that price." He said, "Okay."

We flipped a coin to see who'd set the price. He won the toss. He wrote a figure on a piece of paper and handed it to Jeff, who then handed it to Jim, who then handed it to me. There were some things about the business that he knew that I didn't. It had some problems. But at any rate, I just pulled out my checkbook and wrote him a check and said, "Jim can take care of the stock transfer, which was for everything we owned together. It included Lambert & Winton, Inc., L&W Service Company and whatever inventory we had. I continued to operate my homebuilding business under the Lambert and Winton name for a number of years even though Denton and I were no longer partners.

I have nothing but the highest respect for Denton. In fact he worked for me several years later in Midland, Texas, to supervise and build houses for me.

By that time he was divorced.

We ran into some problems with our business in Albuquerque. We also had a guy working for us named Jake Burnett. He had a degree in accounting and had been in the ready-mix concrete business for himself for years. He was not doing so well when we found him. He was depressed and downhearted. We hired him and put him to running L&W Service and he just blossomed. He was a burly, boisterous guy and having something to manage was his style. So the first thing I told him was, "Jake, you go to Albuquerque and find out everything you can about that business and see where we stand."

So he went there and took it over and we began closing it down because we had some unhappy customers and other kinds of problems.

One day when I had just come in from Albuquerque dealing with some of those problems, I needed Velma Beach, our secretary, to take some dictation to send some letters to Luther G. Branham, the FHA regional director. It was lunch time and no one was at the office except for a new receptionist. I introduced myself and she said she was Connie Stead. She asked if she could help, since Velma was not there. I said I had some important letters that needed to go out, but I would wait until Velma returned. She insisted she could take dictation and so I quickly dictated the letters. I went to the bathroom and when I came back to my desk, there were the three letters on my desk, all perfect. The address was correct, the words were exactly what I said, the spelling was perfect, the punctuation was dead-on. I walked back to the front of the office as if I had seen a ghost and said, "Who are you? I cannot believe you just did that." She said she was in Clovis because her husband was stationed there with the Air Force. I asked how much we were paying her. She told me. I said, "You are worth a lot more than that."

"I know that and I will be leaving as soon as I get a better job."

I told her, "You just found that better job."

There was more talent, ability, efficiency and judgment wrapped in that tiny, cute female than I had ever encountered before. She became my right hand person for the next four years and was a huge contributor to my success in those days. We are still friends and communicate often.

REMEMBER TO THINK *of your life as a plot of rich soil waiting to be seeded. It can return to you only that which you sow. And what do you have to sow? From your God-given riches: You have a mind; you can think; you have many abilities; you have talents that you still may not have explored; and you have time, which cannot be saved, stopped, or held back for a second. Make full use of these riches. It's never too late.*

—EARL NIGHTINGALE

PART V

Loyalty

"An honest politician is one who, when he is bought, will stay bought."

—SIMON CAMERON

Twenty-two

Marty, Jack and Jack

How I got to know Marty Shaeffer is an interesting story. Not too long after I had gone into the business of selling real estate, I had been working out of a real estate office that was next door to a restaurant. I was going into the restaurant one day and met with a fellow I had gone to high school with named Eugene Glidewell. He had with him Marty Shaeffer, who was new to town. He had come as the manager of the telephone company, Mountain Bell, one of the biggest employers in Clovis.

That was a very brief meeting. It turned out that the Shaeffers rented a home next door to my sister Bette and her husband, Howard Cox, the grocery man. Mrs. Shaeffer—Ellen Claire—became acquainted with my sister Bette and they became lifelong friends.

My next meeting with Marty was some time later when a Mountain Bell employee named Bruce Guffey was transferred to a different town, leaving his wife, Dawn, in Clovis to dispose of their home. The telephone company had a program, and still does, where if the house doesn't sell within a certain period of time, the company would buy it from the employee. So I had an offer on their house and I took it to Dawn Guffey. She called her husband to discuss it and he said, "Well I'm not really in a position to make that decision. But I have the greatest respect for Marty Shaeffer, so have him look over that contract and he'll know what to do. He'll know how to compare and make a correct decision about it."

So she called and said, "Marty Shaeffer has agreed to be at my home at five-thirty this afternoon, to talk about the contract, can you come then?" It was a beautiful day, so we sat outside on the patio and I made the contract presentation and told him why I thought it was the right price and so on and so forth. Marty said, "Well, I agree. Dawn, go ahead and sign the contract." Just when we were about to leave she said, "Would you guys like a drink?" And we said, "Well, yeah, it's six-thirty. It's got to be cocktail time somewhere." She made us a drink and left us alone except every once in a while she'd come out and refill our drinks. So we sat there until about ten-thirty at night and became very well acquainted—and the relationship has lasted over forty years.

> *There's a story about a young preacher that was out visiting his flock and he goes to see this elderly senior citizen lady. He sits down in her living room with her, and he sees a little bowl of peanuts there on the table. So, they're talking and he helps himself to the peanuts, and they talk some more. It occurs to him as he's about ready to leave that he had eaten all of the lady's peanuts. He said, "Well, Miss Brown, I'm so sorry. I sat right here and ate all your peanuts."*
>
> *She said, "Oh, that's okay, I had already sucked the chocolate off all of them."*

Not too long after Marty came to Clovis, he was promoted again. He had a bachelor's degree from Brigham Young University and a master's degree from Arizona State University, and when he went to work for the phone company he was selected to be part of a management-training team designed to develop young executives to be top management someday. Among other things, they signed a contract that they would allow their careers to be monitored for twenty-five years by the company, no matter what they did, even if they left the phone company. He had come to Clovis from Silver City, New Mexico, where he had been the manager of that very small exchange, and then he worked in Clovis for a couple of years. During his first tenure in Clovis he built a couple of houses in his spare time.

Then they made him chief of the internal auditing section of a whole group of offices with headquarters in Denver. When he moved to Denver, he was replaced by Jack Dailey, who was in the same program of advancement. So naturally, I never did sell a house to Marty Shaeffer but I did sell one to Jack Dailey and that's how we became friends. Later, when Dailey left the phone company he came to work with me.

One evening, Lunell and I were having dinner with our close friends, Bill and Marge Brack. Bill was the superintendent of the Santa Fe Railroad. We were having dinner with them at the Holiday Inn, where we often ate. The hostess came to me and said, "You have a phone call." There were no cell phones in those days, and I couldn't imagine who it was, so I got on the phone. It was Jack Dailey and he was slurring his words but he said, "Hey you sumbitch get your ass over to my house as soon as you can."

I said, "Well I'm having dinner,"

He said, "Are you finished?"

"Well, just about."

"Get over here."

When we left the restaurant, I had my wife drop me at his house. I said, "I'll have him bring me home." So I walked in and Marty and Jack were sitting straddle-legged in the middle of the floor with a bottle of scotch. They announced to me that Marty had decided he wanted to leave the phone company, move back to Clovis and build homes. He eventually did that, not immediately, but he eventually did.

The difference between a drunk and an alcoholic is the drunk doesn't have to go to all those meetings.

I had two or three years in the real estate business by then so I helped Marty get started by taking him to the bank and introducing him to Mr. Willmon who listened very attentively and then said, "Well, what do you have in mind?"

Marty said, "Well, I'd like to build a couple of houses out in Colonial Park and sell 'em." Colonial Park was a new golf course community and country club on 640 acres in northeast Clovis.

So Mr. Willmon said, "Well, fine, we'll provide financing for you." And so that's how Marty got into the homebuilding business full time.

A man died and went to heaven. St. Peter asked, "I gotta ask you this. How many times did you cheat on your wife in your life?"

He said, "Oh, never. Never, not once."

"Okay. Your reward will be you get to go out in this beautiful Lincoln town car all the time here in heaven."

So, he took it and left. It wasn't too long after that St. Peter happened to notice this car was parked; the man was leaning on the steering wheel crying. St. Peter said, "What's happened? You should be the happiest guy in the world. You can go anywhere you want in this beautiful car."

The guy said, "Yeah, but I just saw my wife go by on a skateboard."

In 1968 or '69, even though I was still partnered with Denton in homebuilding, I started on a project with Marty Shaeffer and Jack Dailey. We formed a partnership called Dailey, Shaeffer & Winton, Inc. That was when we really started making money in land development.

Marty Shaeffer, myself and Jack Dailey, Colonial Park, circa 1970.

Marty had good luck with the homes he built at Colonial Park. The more we thought about it, the more it seemed that developing Colonial into a regular golf course community would be a good idea. Two very fine Baptist gentlemen, Cotton Simms and Dr. I. D. Johnson, owned the subdivision which had a nine-hole golf course.

It was strictly a family club. The owners didn't believe in drinking and dancing. The strongest thing they served there was soda pop and the only food they served there were hamburgers cooked on a grill. In fact, Marty now has that old grill at his fishing camp in Colorado.

Still, the owners recognized the promise in our new young company so they made a deal with us to market all the lots in Colonial Park Development. They gave Dailey, Shaeffer & Winton a very decent contract. They said they'd pay us ten percent of the selling price on the first five lots that we sold in a year, and then it would go to fifteen percent for everything up to ten lots in a year. Anything over that, they would give us twenty percent of the sales price, just for selling the lots.

Marty, Dailey and I were kindred spirits. When you find people in life that you automatically relate to, you become very close. We lived next door to the Shaeffers in Colonial Park. About six one morning, the phone rang.

"Guess what?" I recognized Marty's voice.

"Marty, it's six in the morning…"

"I'm at the hospital. We have a new baby boy!"

"Congratulations," I said.

"Oh, by the way, my car was nearly out of gas so I took yours." Clovis was the kind of place you could leave your keys in the car, and Marty was the kind of friend I didn't mind taking it.

> *My granddaughter, Aleksa, tells me quite a few stories. One of the recent ones she told me was this: A little boy goes to school and says to his teacher, "Teacher, does God live in the bathroom?"*
>
> *She said, "No. I don't think so. Why would you ask that?"*
>
> *He said, "Well, every morning my dad bangs on the door and says, 'Oh, God. Are you still in there?'"*

We used to discuss what our future life should be like. And what we would be willing to give up in order to have the business successes we were looking for. We even bought records on hypnosis and Marty and Dailey and I used to lie on the floor in my office and listen to these records, which were designed to hypnotize you and program your mind for outstanding success.

We also had a lot of fun together. The three of us used to drive to Albuquerque quite often to visit the FHA office. The homes I was building with Denton Lambert were always financed by the FHA, so I always had a reason to go to Albuquerque. Dailey and Shaeffer didn't need a reason. They had both previously lived there.

I remember one time we drove there in a terrible snow storm that nobody had any business being out in. We grabbed us a cold six pack and made it all the way to Santa Rosa, New Mexico, where we got another six pack. We were driving in Marty's station wagon because his tires had steel studs built into them and could handle the icy roads. But the car was so warm that the beer got hot. I remember we put some beer up top in the luggage carrier just for five miles or so, and when we took it down, the beers were all frozen.

The accomplishments of a lifetime are determined by what we get done today. A successful life is achieved by putting successful days together, one day at a time. A successful person is not someone who does not have problems, but someone who has learned to solve those problems.

Twenty-three

Country Club Living

EACH OF US, Marty Schaeffer, Jack Dailey and myself, built ourselves a new home in the subdivision. We all moved into Colonial Park and did very well until Dailey decided he wanted to move back to Albuquerque. He had gone to the University of New Mexico in Albuquerque where he played the opposite half back position to Don Perkins, who later became a big star with the Dallas Cowboys. Dailey and "Perk," as he called him, were bosom buddies. Dailey's wife was also from Albuquerque and she had family there. He was the big football star and she was the cheerleader. So he took off to Albuquerque.

Dailey says that the training he got and all the motivational material that I made my people listen to was important to him. He started a real estate company in Albuquerque that became one of the largest in the city. He eventually sold it and now does commercial real estate brokerage. Eventually Jack Dailey remarried to one of the most intelligent and funny women I have ever met named Elaine. She is an attorney practicing law in Albuquerque and we are always exchanging jokes. We both try to find jokes the other has not heard. One time I told her, "Elaine, that joke is so old, I kicked a slat out of my crib the first time I heard it." She thought that was funnier than the joke she had just told me. We enjoy visiting and traveling with them whenever we can all match our schedules.

We enjoyed Colonial Park and life in Clovis. Todd, my third son, was twelve or thirteen years old when he got a job working at the golf course cleaning clubs at the pro shop. Andy, Scott and Jeff all became excellent golfers. Scott says that even though he may not play golf much anymore, when he gets together with Andy (who himself may not have played for years), Andy always beats him with a near-par game. I personally never took up golf. I tried it a few times, but I didn't have the patience for it.

Ultimately, Marty and I proposed to the two owners of the subdivision that they sell us the whole subdivision, the golf course and the country club. It was 640 acres of land, including several lots that were developed and ready to use. We negotiated on that deal for a month or so. They were perfectly willing to sell. They didn't want it and they certainly didn't want it without us. We made a very attractive deal to buy the whole operation from them.

I had been receiving a fee from a mortgage company in Roswell for giving them the business of our FHA homes. My secretary Velma Beach was an absolute whiz at processing FHA loans. We put the loans together for this bank in Roswell, gave them the loans to submit to the FHA, and then closed on the loans while keeping the fees that come with them. The Roswell bank retained the servicing of those loans. I was collecting a half percent on each loan. I had no particular need for that money, so I was just rat-holing it, putting it into Certificates of Deposit. When the opportunity came along to buy Colonial Park, Marty didn't have a lot of cash, but I had that money in CDs in Citizens Bank, so that was what we used as our down payment.

We hired a golf pro by the name of Ray Hardy and expanded the nine hole course into an eighteen hole course. Ray and his wife Wanda managed the golf course and the newly-remodeled clubhouse. We added dramatically to the clubhouse by building a big dining room that sat two hundred people for shows and dinner dances. Everybody started having their weddings and their receptions at our country club.

To promote our club, we bought an addressograph machine that could send out four hundred postcards in an hour and a half. We asked the chefs and the manager, "What's the worst day of the week?" On Thursday we had less business, less food sold, less bar business, less everything. So we began promoting a Thursday evening Mexican fiesta, starting out with margaritas for forty-nine cents between five and seven o'clock. Whereas we used to serve eight or nine meals on a Thursday night, suddenly we were serving forty-five or fifty. I bought a beautifully embroidered Mexican suit and a serape and sombrero. I would wear the suit and go around to the tables and tell the waiters, "Give these people another round," like they do in Cancun. In Cancun, they give you free shots of tequila up to a point and then you wind up spending fifty dollars, once they have you lubricated. That's kind of what I did at the club, and I would stay at the club until late into the night. I had fun being the club clown.

> *Two golfers were having breakfast and one of them was reading the newspaper. He said, "I see that a man beat his wife to death with an eight iron."*
> *His buddy asked, "How many strokes did it take?"*

Marty and I were paid a salary through the land development company that allowed us to live comfortably. I could keep profits that I was generating from the homebuilding company and L&W Service—and Jack Winton Realty before I sold it. We even went into the swimming pool manufacturing business and landscaping business. We had a fellow named Leo Shaw who ran that company. So I owned, or had interests in, companies that did electrical, plumbing, heating and cooling, swimming pools, land development, homebuilding and real estate. All of those different things in Clovis, not a one by itself was a particularly lucrative business, but combined, they made a very comfortable living. We would set up a new company for everything and make it self-sufficient.

I didn't realize it but I was following the advice that Mr. Campbell of Campbell Industries in Clovis had given me years before, when I was in the military. I was selecting the right people and turning it over to them and always being available to talk and discuss and to help with major decisions. But basically I left them alone on the day to day operation, letting them run it.

Give me some men who are stout-hearted men
Who will fight for the right they adore.
Start me with ten, who are stout-hearted men
And I'll soon give you ten thousand more.

Oh! Shoulder to shoulder and bolder and bolder
They grow as they go to the fore!
Then there's nothing in the world can halt or mar a plan,
When stout-hearted men can stick together man to man!

You who have dreams,
If you act, they will come true.
Would you turn your dreams to a fact.
It's up to you.

If you have the soul and the spirit,
Never fear it, you'll see it through.
Hearts can inspire other hearts with their fire,
For the strong obey when a strong man
Shows them the way.

From the song "Stout-Hearted Men" by Romberg and Hammerstein, first performed in the operetta *The New Moon*.

Twenty-four

My Life in a Cardboard Box

Lunell and I had four boys in six years, Andy, Scott, Todd and Jeff. Their mother, bless her heart, had a handful trying to raise them without any help from her husband. She warned me repeatedly, "I can't keep going on like this. I can't keep doing this," I guess I didn't take her seriously.

I hate to say it, but during a pretty substantial portion of my life, I kind of neglected my family. I was concentrating on other things, not the least of which was business. But I was also meeting my buddies at the Gold Lantern and maybe pinching a waitress or two. I could have been a better husband.

I came home from work one night about nine o'clock. The outside light was on, and there were two cardboard boxes sitting on the front porch. There was a note on one of the boxes. I picked up the paper and read, *This is your stuff. I've had the locks changed on the house, filed for divorce and if you try to come in, I'll call the police.*

We got married in 1953 and I think the divorce finally became final in 1972. We were separated for a year or more while the attorneys attempted to unravel the details. Anyway, Lunell is a fine person and I have the utmost respect for her and an appreciation for her being a good mother to our sons.

> *There was a terrible storm and all of the creeks and rivers were rising. A man was standing on his porch as some men came paddling by in a row boat. They said, "Get in, the flood waters are rising." The man said, "No I will wait here, God will save me." A short time later they came by again, but this time the waters were lapping at the eaves of the house and the man was sitting up on the peak of the roof. They again told him to get in because the flood waters were still rising. He again said no, that God would save him.*
>
> *A short time later he was in the upper branches of a tree and the water was at his ankles. The row boat came by again and they said, "Get in man, the flood waters are still rising, you are in danger of drowning." He again told them, "God will save me."*
>
> *The waters did continue to rise and the man drowned. When he got to heaven he asked God, "Why didn't you save me?" God said, "I sent you a boat three times."*

That night I took the boxes a few blocks away to a model home in the subdivision. It all looked very nice so I went into the master bedroom and pulled the bedspread back, and of course there's no sheets. There's no mattress pad. There's nothing on it. It's just all for show. I don't think we even had the gas turned on. So I slept on the mattress that night and took a cold shower the next morning using the display towels, and then went to the office. Later when I opened up the box, I found two saucers, two cups, two plates, some of my underwear and not much else.

I guess she thought I was expecting company.

But being in the building business, we had units available and I selected one and set about to turn it into a home, a place to live that was part of the Colonial development. I flew the plane to El Paso, went and visited some furniture stores and ordered furnishings and had them shipped to Clovis. I made some pretty good deals just by offering: "Write this all up right now and I'll write you a check right now." So, they came with a big truck and unloaded it, and we put everything in place.

That little house worked out very well. It was Number 3 Paseo Village. Paseo Village was a freestanding, zero-lot-line patio home project that Marty and I collaborated on. I built all of the odd-numbered houses. He built the even ones. It had, I believe, thirty-nine units in it.

It was a nice little place. It had its own community swimming pool and a playground area and so on. It is very successful even right now. We were selling those homes for twenty-five to thirty-five thousand dollars. Today the same houses are going for about $150,000. Nothing like that had ever been built in Clovis. Marty and I saw the concept in Arizona, and thought we would try it in Clovis. We had a hard time getting it approved by the city because we had a neighbor organize a protest against it. She was trying to instill a fear in the neighbors and city commission that small lots and smaller houses would create a future slum. We felt there was a market for an alternative type of housing that wasn't being offered in Clovis. It was approved though and proved to be very desirable for the market and the predictions of the protestors have been shown to be unfounded.

So, anyway, that's where I settled in for a pretty good spell. And then we came up with a new project that fronted along the golf course. And the first one was built for me. It was just dandy, a real bachelor pad.

Money can't buy happiness,
but it sure makes misery
easier to live with.

Dr. Lynn Abshere and myself playing raquet ball at Colonial Park.

Marty and I, in our country club, built a handball and racquetball court. He played handball and I played racquetball, each with a selection of enthusiastic friends. Everybody had to call the club to reserve a time for the court and you couldn't make a reservation earlier than eight a.m. for a same day reservation. One of Connie's jobs was make my reservation. She'd watch that second hand and make the call and had that court reserved just about every day at five o'clock. So I would wind up playing about twenty-eight days a month. She would call up someone from a list she kept and get someone to play with me, so I didn't know who I was going to play. I became quite fit after all that practice.

One time, I was playing with a fellow who said, "I'm really going to clean your plate." I said, "I'll tell you what I'll do. I'll give you thirteen out of the fifteen points before we start the game." Then I asked him, "Which hand do you want me to play with?"

I sometimes played racquetball with a guy named Ben Abruzzo, who along with Maxie Anderson went across the Atlantic Ocean in a hot air balloon called the Double Eagle II. It was a world event at the time because no one had ever done it.

Ben owned a shopping center in Clovis that he'd check in on from time to time. We'd go to lunch and play racquetball; then he'd fly back to Albuquerque. One day I was favoring my left arm because I had developed a bad tennis elbow in my right arm.

"Oh, what's the matter?"

"I've got tennis elbow," I said.

"Oh, Jack, I know the best orthopedic surgeon that's ever been, right in Albuquerque. I'll give him a call."

There was a phone on the wall in the locker room and he went over and called and said, "Hello John, this is Ben. I'm over here in Clovis and I've got a friend with a bad elbow. I'm gonna bring him into your office this afternoon. Don't leave until I get there." So I'm sitting here watching all this big-eyed. He says, "Do you have to take anything with you?"

I said, "I don't know. Where am I going?"

"I'm taking you to Albuquerque to see this doctor."

"Well, let's swing by the house so I can get my shaving gear."

I still didn't believe what was happening, but sure enough, we got into his plane and took off for Albuquerque.

We landed and went straight to John's office. He X-rayed my arm while Ben sat out in the waiting room. The doctor called me in and said, "First of all let me say you know Ben's crazy, don't you?"

"Well, I know he's a little unusual."

"I've known him for years, and he's crazy. Yes you have a requirement for surgery. It's strictly elective; you can do it any time. Why don't you let me know when you can make arrangements that won't interfere with your life and your business and we can take care of it?"

I said, "Actually, now that I'm here, couldn't you do it in the morning?"

"My God, you're as crazy as Ben."

> *A fella went to the psychiatrist for examination. After being examined, he sat down with the doctor, and the doctor said, "Well, I hate to tell you this, but you're crazy." The patient said, "Well, I want a second opinion." The doctor looked at him and said, "Okay. You're ugly too."*

The next morning he operated on my elbow and I was out all afternoon with anesthesia. Marty Shaeffer happened to be in Albuquerque, building homes, and he dropped by the hospital in the afternoon. I was just coming out of it, and he said, "Where's your clothes?"

"Why?"

"Come on, let's get out of here."

He looked in the closet and found my clothes and I said, "I have to talk to the doctor and get released."

"Well, they won't release you."

"So what do you suggest?"

And he said, "I know a back door out of this place. Let's get you dressed and get out of here."

And we did. Flying back it was one hundred degrees and we were bouncing all over the sky and I had laid the seat back and all of sudden I said, "Marty I'm going to be sick."

"Well, let me get you a barf bag."

He didn't get it in time and I was there barfing all over the back of the airplane. Marty was helping me hold the barf bag with one hand and flying the plane with the other. When we landed, I was looking around in the back seat and he said, "Well what are you doing looking around back there?"

"I've lost my contact lens." I finally found it after sorting through the prior contents of my stomach that were now on the airplane floor. There is really nothing like the smell of vomit in a one hundred degree Cessna. I always admired Marty for having been willing and able to suffer through that. I guess his old Navy days on a submarine helped him out there.

What is money? Money is the harvest of our production. Money is what we receive for our production and service to others, which we can then use to obtain the production and services of others.

—EARL NIGHTINGALE

Twenty-five

Joy

Business was going gangbusters at Colonial Development. Both Shaeffer Homes and Lambert & Winton were developing lots of properties at Colonial Park, and I had good people running my other enterprises. Jake Burnett was running L&W Service Company, Leo Shaw was running the swimming pool and landscaping company and Marty was there looking after the land development business.

I sold Jack Winton Realty to a father and two sons who worked for me. Bill and Gene Echols both worked for me when their father, Coy Echols, sold Murphy-Echols Tire Company that he had run for forty years. Soon after Coy also came to work for me. He was a very smooth, successful and impressive individual. I eventually sold him and his sons the business. Everybody in town thought I had hit a home run, but they didn't understand the deal.

Someone asked, "What is a real estate company? You don't own anything; you rent the building and you own the office furniture."

I explained, "Yes but we also have a file of transactions that will close." I thought they made a good deal and I was happy with it. I believe that if a deal is good for only one party, it is not a good deal. I think it has to be a good deal for all parties concerned. The Echols kept the signage, the colors, everything exactly the same, but later they changed the name to Echols Realty. I started a little company called Colonial Realty.

Marty and his wife E. C. had built a large home at 921 Colonial Parkway which was the first structure you saw as you entered the Colonial Park subdivision. We thought that with its commanding views of the golf course it would be an ideal location for our offices. I was a single guy working in my new office, which was on our golf course looking over the number one green and the number two tee box, a block and a half from our clubhouse where I played racquetball every day at five o'clock in the afternoon.

Jeff Jacobs, a CPA who had retired after twenty-nine years of running his own firm, was working for us. He had been my accountant way back when in the meat packing business and had recently sold his practice to another firm. Jeff and his wife, Billie, were good friends and regulars at the country club. They liked to play golf and they participated in club activities. So I suggested to Jeff that he needed to have a place to go and have something to do. "Would you like to come out here and work for us in our beautiful home on the golf course? You can have a private office and help us with our accounting."

He became the office manager. One day he came to me and said, "We need a receptionist. Our receptionist is leaving."

I said, "Why don't you just hire one?"

"How do you propose I go about it?"

"You ran an accounting office for twenty-nine years?" I asked.

"Yes."

"What did you do when you needed a receptionist?"

"I ran an ad in the paper and called an employment office."

I suggested, not so politely, that maybe the same strategy could work in this situation.

He was right down the hall from me, but one morning about ten o'clock he called me on the intercom, "Jack I'm interviewing this girl for the receptionist job, I'd like you to meet her."

I said, "Oh, Okay."

He said, "This is Marla Milsap," and I said, "Nice to meet you."

Then at about eleven-thirty he said, "Jack I've been interviewing this girl and I'd like for you to meet her. She's been working at McDonald's, she'd like to be our receptionist."

I went over and said, "Okay. Nice to meet you."

About two o'clock he calls again and says, "Jack I'm interviewing this girl to be our receptionist and I'd like for you to meet her."

And I said, "Jeff, do you think that you have sense enough to hire a receptionist?"

"Well, yeah, why?"

"Then damnit it, do it and leave me alone."

At about five he called and said, "Jack I'm interviewing this girl for a receptionist. I'd like you to meet her."

I went storming down the hall, jerked the door open. There's Jeff in this three piece suit and tie, sitting behind his big old desk. And sitting in a chair is a little, tiny, blonde lady with short hair who has her legs crossed and her foot swinging. She has all the right parts in all the right places. Jeff said, "Jack, This is Joy. She is looking for a job as a receptionist." I never took my eyes off her.

"Give her the job."

Jeff said, "She says she doesn't type very well."

"No problem. We can work around that."

"She also says she's not going to work somewhere where the only thing she has to do is jump around and bring the guys coffee."

"No problem, no problem. We can get our own coffee."

"I guess the worst part is. She will not start at minimum wage."

I said, "That's Okay. Pay her whatever she wants. So I get up and I say, "I will see you later."

I leave Jeff's office. Probably ten minutes later, Jeff comes into my office with a grin on his face and says, "Jack I have never been so embarrassed in all my life."

"Who embarrassed you?"

"Why, you did."

"I embarrassed you? How?"

"The way you acted with that girl there."

"How much did you have to pay her to get her to come to work?"

"I didn't hire her. I have two more appointments for that receptionist job."

I said, "Jeff, if she's not here at eight o'clock tomorrow morning, you are fired."

That's how I met Joy.

Joy's perspective:

I didn't last very long working as Jack's receptionist. He scared me to death. But the interesting part of this whole story was Jack always played racquetball every day at 5:00. He was the champion racquetball player at the club. Nobody could beat him. I mean he'd hit one ball and stand in the middle of the court with those dangerous elbows. Nobody could get around him. Nobody could score. He beat everybody. So the receptionist's job—she didn't have to do anything else, literally—was to get him a racquetball match every day at 5:00. Now isn't it strange that the only day he's in the office at 5:00, and not playing racquetball, is when I came for an interview?

Anyway, I really needed work. I had been looking for a job, and I hadn't found one yet. I had been a dental assistant but not a big deal. And I really had only had one year of college, married my high school sweetheart, been with him forever, had two little girls, and then we divorced.

It was late. It was almost 5:00, but I stopped at the employment agency and said, "I really need a job. Is there anything?"

The lady at the agency said, "Honey, you know what I think—why don't you run out to the Colonial Park Country Club real estate office."

I said, "I don't even know where it is."

She said, "It's close. Let me just call and see if somebody's there?" And she said, "Sure enough, Jeff Jacobs is there."

And so she had me run out there. Now, Jack would normally not be there at 5:00 p.m. but was there that day.

After Jack came into the interview, he sat down and didn't look at anything else the whole time he was there, just right at me. It literally scared me to death. I didn't know what to think.

Upon reflection, I don't know how I came up with all that stuff about not working for minimum wage or serving coffee. I mean, I literally had to have a job. After Jack left the room, having no idea who that crazy nut was, I looked over at the guy with the suit behind the desk and I said, "I don't know who that guy was but you don't have to hire me just because of what he said." And I was still shaking. I just knew I didn't get the job.

Jeff said, "Well, I really appreciate that attitude." He said, "I do have more people to interview in the morning."

So I went to my car and I just busted out crying thinking I was so worthless, and I couldn't even get a job as a receptionist. I cried all the way home.

Then when I got home, Mr. Jacobs was calling on my phone saying, "Joy, can you be here at eight in the morning?" And I said, "Oh my goodness, yes, yes, I'll be there."

Well, as soon as I hit the door at my new job the next morning, Jack said, "Want to go to lunch today?"

I said, "No. No. No, not ever."

Now I didn't have any idea about country clubs—I had never even been in a country club, much less known anybody that owned a country club. And he kept asking me and I kept saying no, no, no. I was very cautious about him.

Then all these girls started appearing out of the woodwork, dropping by, "Oh, honey, can you run back and get Mr. Winton's credit card? He needs new placemats at his house." I said, sure, and I'd run back, "Jack, Jean's here and she wants your credit card for placemats." He said, "Oh sure," just whipped it out, "Here you go." In the meantime, he had all these other women coming and going like crazy.

I remember one day I was sitting there and this little old lady came in. I am a sympathetic person by nature—whatever your problem is I'm gonna

Joy with Kristel and Monica about the time we met. Joy was driving my "bachelor" Corvette convertible that day.

help you. I cry with you or whatever. Well, this precious little old lady came hobbling in, and Jack was right there. He had been out there working on me to go to lunch. He was sitting across the room in the receptionist area, and the lady was between us. She said, "Honey, I came in to see Mr. Winton." I said, "Okay," but he's just sitting behind her shaking his head "No" and scribbling furiously on a notepad. And I said, "Well, he's, uh, uh, can you come back if I make an appointment?" She said, "Well, I guess so." And I was looking at Jack bewildered. He wouldn't see this poor little lady. So I sat there listening to her whole story. And in the middle of that he was still writing a note that said, "Well, if you won't have lunch with me, will you at least have dinner with me?" I think I was the only female who ever told him "NO" on all accounts!

> *An elderly farmer married a good looking, voluptuous young bride, and he brought her home. And, after a few weeks they went to visit the doctor. He said, "We're really having some problems in bed. I can be out plowing, driving the tractor, and start thinking about her. And, I just get so excited. And then at night when I'm in bed with her I just can't do anything."*
>
> *The doctor said, "Okay, here's what I want you to do—both of you. When you have those urges and you're driving the tractor, you disconnect that plow, and you come charging home just as fast as that tractor will go."*
>
> *And, to her, "You keep an eye out. And when you see him coming, take off all your clothes and jump in bed and be ready for him."*
>
> *A few days later, she looks up and his tractor is just bouncing along, and really, really going fast, heading to the house. He jumps off of it and runs in, and sees her in bed and, he says, "Get out of bed, you sex maniac. The house is on fire."*

Joy finally relented and went out with me. But I learned that I was dealing with a strong-minded woman.

One time Joy was going with me to Juárez, Mexico, with Ellen Claire and Marty. Ellen Claire was off doing something and Marty and I and Joy were sitting at a bar at ten or eleven in the morning and we were having a beer.

I was lighting a cigarette and Joy said, "Why don't you stop smoking?"

I said, "Why don't you stop wearing a bra?"

"I will, if you stop smoking."

"I will." I said.

So Joy, who is very well endowed, reached up under her blouse and pulls this bra out and throws it in the trash can over behind the bar. I took my cigarettes and threw them in the trash can too. And she said, "Is that the last you are going to smoke?"

I said, "Yes. I promise."

Three weeks later, at a dinner party I gave, I'm sitting there with the guys telling stories and Joy is there. I pull a cigarette from someone's pack on the table and I light it. I hadn't smoked one in three weeks. So I'm sitting there with everybody. And Joy is putting her coat on and saying, "Thank you, I had a good time."

And I said, "What's the deal?"

"I'm leaving. I don't have any use for somebody that promises me something and then doesn't do it."

She goes out the door and slams it.

That just pissed me off something fierce. She wouldn't talk to me for three days, so I thought, I'll rely on my friend Marty Shaeffer. He'll take up for me. I finally got a hold of Marty and told him the problem and I said, "Isn't that ridiculous?" and he said, "Well, not necessarily. She felt strongly that you made a promise and didn't keep it. I can understand her point of view."

I said, "You no good, sorry ass."

I called Joy to apologize and said, "If you will overlook my mistake, I'll never smoke again." And that was almost forty years ago.

Joy's perspective:

I was raised in a little farmhouse with six kids. There were my three brothers, Ronnie, Butch and Craig and my two sisters Donna and Jan. We were wall-to-wall mattresses with the six kids and Mother and Daddy sleeping on the back porch. And my daddy was a little cowboy before it was cool, as were my brothers. So he would wake up every morning, start his cigarettes and country music. I grew up hating the smell of cigarettes. He passed away from emphysema at an early age, strictly because of cigarettes.

As our relationship progressed, we were under the scrutiny of our country club set. I would take Joy there for dinner and dancing every Friday night, and we would come back to my bachelor pad on the golf course. She would spend the night, and you might not believe this, but I would sleep upstairs and she would sleep downstairs on this huge water bed that I had.

That very first Saturday morning at about eight-thirty her dad called. He said, "Hey Jack, is Joy with you?"
"Yes, sir, she is."
He said, "Well let me ask you something. "What's y'all's plans?"
"Oh, we're going to play tennis with some people at eleven o'clock and then about noon we'll go into the club house and have a lunch and then probably go swimming."
And he said, "Okay, thank you," and hung up.
Well a week or two later, she spent the night again. Saturday morning, about eight-thirty, the phone rang. "Hello?"
He said, "Jack, this here's Dub Chumley."
I said, "Good morning, Mr. Chumley."
"Is Joy over there?"
"Well, yes sir, she is. You want to talk to her?"
"Nope, but I got a question for you."
"What is it?"
"What's y'all's plans? And I ain't talking about playing tennis and going swimming."
We got married shortly after that. She was twenty-three. I was thirty-nine, about to turn forty.

Did you hear about the letter to Dear Abby? It read, "Dear Abby, I have a fiancé. We're very much in love with each other. He's asked me to marry him and I want your advice about what I should do. My father is serving a life sentence for murder. My mother is serving her third term in jail for prostitution. My sister is following in the steps of my mother, and my younger brother is in reform school for drug distribution. Now I told him all those things and he says it doesn't make any difference. However, I have a third cousin who's a land developer. Should I tell him?"

Joy's mom, also named Joy, was a little more tolerant than Dub, I think. She became one of my biggest fans, and I one of hers. I am a real connoisseur of home-style country cooking, and I must say that in her heyday, Joy's mom was probably one of the very best cooks who ever existed. Everything and anything she cooked was absolutely delicious, and I particularly remember her chocolate cream pies. We arrived at their house one evening from El Paso, and she had just made a chocolate pie. I sat down at the table and ate half the pie all by myself in one sitting. She's a wonderful person and a wonderful cook and is a big support and help to me in everything I do.

Most accidents happen at home.
And the men have to eat them!

We built the membership of the club up to where we had four hundred dues-paying members, and we built one new tennis court, resurfaced the existing one and started a tennis program. That's where Joy came into the picture. She had never played tennis before but she was a natural so she helped promote the program. It wasn't too long until we had fifty people out there to watch tennis matches we had arranged between the top players on Sunday afternoons. It was an interesting and fun time.

Before we got married I said to Joy one day, "Now, look, I have risen to a certain level in the world, you know, and I've been around a few

Madeline "Joy" Chumley, Joy's mother, and one of my biggest fans.

goat ropings and a couple of county fairs or whatever."

"So I need to make something clear that you understand. I'll be the colonel and you can be the private. What you have to learn to do is say 'yes sir, no sir, and no excuse sir.' Do you think that's going to be a problem?"

She said, "No problem whatsoever. I can handle that." So we got married, and about fifteen years later, one day I said, "Do you happen to remember that conversation we had about me being the colonel and you being the private?"

She said, "Oh, I remember it very well."

"You were supposed to have learned to say 'yes sir, no sir, and no excuse sir' and that's all. What happened to that idea?"

She said, "Hey, you're still a colonel, always have been. How was I to know I was going to be promoted to general?"

Successful people follow independent paths. They break away from the crowd. They join a smaller crowd. They don't have the television on all day long. They use their time constructively. Since so few tap their inner potential, it's easier for one to win, There is less competition getting to the top, and the view is better.

—Earl Nightingale

Twenty-six

Green Fingers

When I asked Joy to marry me, we decided on a Sunday morning that we were going to take a trip and we were probably going to get married before it was over, because that's what Joy told her Daddy.

I called my buddy, Dr. Abshere, my flying partner, and said, "Joy and I need a blood test."

He said, "What for? You guys sick?"

"No, we're thinking about possibly getting married." He just laughed and laughed.

He said, "So why are you telling me?"

I said, "Because, you jerk, we need you to meet us at the hospital in about fifteen minutes and give us a blood test." So we got our blood test, then we went to Jack Dailey's house in Albuquerque and had dinner that night at the Beef Wellington restaurant and spent the night.

The next morning we got up, drove down to the county courthouse in Albuquerque, gave them our blood tests and all that, and bought a marriage license. David Norvell, the friend I'd owned the Piper Tri-Pacer with, was now the Attorney General of New Mexico. I called him and said, "David, I presume the people in New Mexico in their infinite wisdom have not seen fit to give you the authority to marry people?"

He laughed and said, "Yes, you're right. They haven't, but why? Who's getting married?"

"Me."

I'd been single for a couple of years and everybody kind of knew that it was a rather interesting lifestyle. He laughed and said, "Come on, tell me it's not true? You're kidding me. This can't be."

"Nah, it's true."

"Well, you got a license?"

"Yeah."

"Do you know Judge Joe Martinez, the Supreme Court Justice?"

"Yeah, I met him at a cocktail party at Jack Dailey's house."

"Come on up to Santa Fe. I'll have him recess the court, step into his chambers, and marry you guys."

"Okay."

So we headed up to David Norvell's office. He said, "Okay, you guys wait right here." He went into the court—the Supreme Court—and whispered to the judge's ear. The judge said, "People, I'm sorry we're gonna have to take a ten minute recess. Something very important has come up." Bam went his gavel.

He came in the office and said, "Hi, Jack, how you doing?" I said, "Fine." He married us. He went back to court. Norvell took us downstairs to some kind of super-duper bar and bought a $150 bottle of champagne for us to celebrate our wedding.

Joy's perspective:

We both said we would never get married, but it wasn't but two weeks later he was asking me, even before he talked with my dad. He would stop the tennis game and get me to the net and ask me to marry him, and I'd say, "Absolutely not. There's just no way." I started to work for him in January and we were married by June. And everybody thought it wouldn't work.

But oh, it's been fabulous. We are still best friends. We still go to lunch every single day together. And we are coming close to our fortieth wedding anniversary.

I got married in my 1970s Kmart mini-dress. Jack wore a huge diamond and I wore a little gold band my mom had given me that I had always had on my hand.

So Jack said, "Well, why don't you just get married with that?"

I said, "Great."

So I got married with my mom's gold band and he got married with his huge diamond ring he had gotten in a trade on a golf course lot and we went on our honeymoon. At a little truck stop, they had a basket of rings at the cash register: $1.78 each.

Jack said, "Come here, honey. Look through those rings. You can have any one you want.

So I picked one with a little pretty silver design on it, and I stuck it on my finger. Well, do you know how nosy those country club women were because they heard Jack was now married? I mean to tell you, we went there every night to dance and as soon as we got there, they'd start approaching me. We would walk in the door and these ladies would just rush at us and say, "Let me look at your ring." And I'd hold up my ring and they'd go, "Ooooh."

I never said a word. Even after my finger turned green I never said a word. I wear a diamond today, but I still have that ring. It's still green. I love that ring, and I wore it forever. I loved it.

Jack came home one day when I was vacuuming, which God forbid if I ever have to do that again, and he said, "Honey, we're going to go down to the jeweler." I said, "What for?" And he said, "Well, we're going to buy your ring." I said, "Well, I don't need a ring. This one is great. I love it." 'Cause I loved looking at the faces of those women when they asked to see my ring.

He took me down to Holmberg Jewelry on Main Street in Clovis to buy a diamond and I'm thinking, a diamond ring, and I'm already ready to go. I've never seen anything called a loose diamond. And he tells Buddy Holmberg, the owner, "Bring out those diamonds that we talked about on the phone please."

So he brings all these diamonds and they're all laid out and he says, "Well, just pick out the one you want."

I said, "Well, I don't know anything about this, you know." So I picked out a little diamond and Jack says, "No, that's not big enough. Buddy, why don't you pick out her diamond?"

So Buddy picks out a beautiful diamond for me. And then I'm thinking, well, okay, what's it gonna look like? I needed a ring. So they ended up getting me a beautiful diamond ring which I still have.

And then we both had nice diamond rings.

> *There were two couples—elderly couples—who always went to dinner together. The two men always rode in the front seat, and the two women in the back seat. They were driving along talking about where they might eat, and the driver says, "Boy, we found a really neat new place to eat. It's an Italian place. The pasta was wonderful—just perfect and fresh. The salads were really crisp, and the price was great."*
>
> *The other guy says, "What's the name of the place?"*
>
> *The driver says, "It's called the, the—what's the name of that flower that has long stems and thorns on it. They're white, and red and yellow?"*
>
> *His friend said, "Rose?"*
>
> *"Yes! That's it!" Then he turned around and said to his wife, "Rose, what's the name of that restaurant?"*

Well, there's a very exclusive dress shop in Clovis called the Vohs Company, and Harry Vohs was the second generation owner. One day I said to Joy, "Go down there and buy you some new clothes." So she goes into the Vohs Company and everybody kind of ignores her for the most part.

Yeah, pretty much like in the movie Pretty Woman. *Finally somebody comes up and says, "Hi there, honey, and who are you?"*

Joy and me on our honeymoon in 1974.

I said, "My name is Joy Winton."

She said, "Oh, you must be Jack's new little daughter-in-law," because Jack's son Andy had just gotten married. He was just a little bit younger than me.

Another clerk said, "You're Lunell's little daughter-in-law, aren't you?" That's Jack's ex-wife.

Eventually the owner finds out who I am and comes out of his office, and asks, "What sort of clothes do you like?" I said, "Well, I don't know, I kind of like this, but on the other hand, I don't know if Jack would like it. I like this. I like this. I like this, this and this." So Harry's gathering up all of these things and he says, "Where are you parked?"

"Well, I'm parked right out here in front of the store, why?"

"Take all these things home and try them on and see what he likes."

"But how am I gonna pay you?"

"Honey, don't worry about it. Just take them and go." So of course, I did.

When we came back from our honeymoon, we resided in my little golf course bachelor pad and then subsequently we had a chance to sell that and we moved into one of our single family homes over in the subdivision. It wasn't backing up to the golf course anymore but it was a nice area. We lived there with our two tiny little girls, two and three years old, Monica and Kristel. And that's where we were living when the Charlie Crowder thing came along, ultimately resulting in our moving to El Paso.

We lived in those two homes for not much over a year. We got married in June of '74 and moved to El Paso in October of '75. So, most of our married life has been in El Paso.

Before Roger Bannister, the great runner and the first person to run a mile under four minutes, everyone knew it was impossible for someone to break the four-minute mile. Yet within weeks of Bannister's record, other runners had beaten it. Since then the record has even been broken in high school events. So what had been perceived as a physical barrier, something that was not physically possible for the human body to do, was actually a psychological barrier.

Twenty-seven

The Newlyweds

MARTY AND I had an airplane and in Clovis, you "ain't nobody" unless you had an airplane. And so Joy and I would fly one weekend to Oklahoma to see my mother and then another weekend to Las Vegas and maybe another weekend to Acapulco or somewhere. And I didn't realize it until later, but I was creating a monster. The first year of our marriage, we took twenty-eight vacations for a total of eighty-three days.

When we got married, I just delighted in surprising Joy. For example, on one of our trips to Las Vegas, after she had begun playing tennis and showing a tremendous interest in it, we popped into a store that specialized in tennis togs. The lady managing the store told us that the owner had a girlfriend who was a size seven, and that he had stocked the whole store with everything in her size. And now the owner decided to sell his business or get a new girlfriend, I don't remember which, and he needed to liquidate inventory. And so, like in a lot of these upscale places, they said, "You sit down over here and we'll bring you a scotch and soda and let her try on some clothes."

So she began trying on these tennis outfits, and I mean this goes on all afternoon. Two hours (and a few adult beverages) later I was beginning

Joy and me with her parents, Joy and Dub Chumley, right before their first airplane flight in 1975.

to think, "How in the hell am I gonna get out of this?" So I said to Joy, "The things you really like you put over here in one pile. The things that you just aren't too crazy about you put over here in another pile."

So there were thirty tennis dresses over here in the pile of what she did like. I said, "Okay," to the clerk. "Here's what I want you to do. Match up each of these with the socks that they wear with the little balls behind, headbands, armbands, and the little panties with the ruffles, and they all need to be color coordinated and match together." I thought I would eliminate at least half of these by doing that.

Not so. She found headbands. Oh, and ruffled panties that matched them and I think it was thirty complete outfits. And then finally at the end, and by now I've had maybe my second or third adult beverage, she said, "Which ones do you want to buy?" And I said, "How many were there that you found everything that went together with it?" And she

Joy and me with Elaine Dailey after a hard tennis match of doubles. Jack Dailey took the picture.

said, "About thirty." I said, "We'll just take 'em all."

We had to go into the same shopping center and buy a huge piece of Samsonite luggage to hold all the outfits to bring them home.

While we were in Las Vegas, we called home to check on the girls. Monica, who was five at the time, answered the phone and the operator asked if she would pay for a collect call. Monica asked, "How much is it? I only have a $1.25."

Later I organized a trip for all of the members of our club who were in the tennis program. We went to the tennis camp held by Rod Laver and Roy Emerson at April Sound, just north of Houston. They had four or five of these camps going on in different parts of the country, tennis lessons with Australian instructors. It happened that the one at April Sound was the last one of the year and the others had been closed down as the season ended. So both Rod Laver and Roy Emerson came and spent the entire week there at our camp. Laver holds the record for most singles titles won in the history of tennis, with two hundred career titles. He is also the only tennis player to have twice won the Grand Slam by winning all four major singles titles in the same year. Roy Emerson is an Australian former World No. 1 tennis player who won twelve Grand Slam tournament singles titles and sixteen Grand Slam tournament men's doubles titles. Roy is the only male player to have won singles and doubles titles at all four Grand Slam events. These two were world class players and this was a world class camp.

Joy wore one outfit in the morning and changed at noon and wore a different one in the afternoon for every day of the week. Both Rod Laver and Roy Emerson were very taken with Joy. The Australians voted her "The Girl They Would Most Like to be Stranded on an Island With."

On the last day of the camp, they traditionally had a mixed doubles match between Roy Emerson and a partner he picked from the attendees against Rod Laver and the partner of his choice. Rod picked Joy to be his partner. So, she got to play tennis as Rod Laver's partner in a mixed doubles.

Two priests go to Aruba on their vacation. They arrive at the hotel and one priest asks, "What's the first thing you want to do on your vacation?"

"Well, I want to take this collar off, get out of these priest clothes, get some touristy looking clothes and not let anybody know we're priests."

So that's what they do; they get some colorful clothes and they're sitting on the beach with a drink, and here comes a good looking gal walking down the beach topless, doesn't have much on the bottom—pretty good looking. She gets up to them and says, "Good afternoon Father, good afternoon Father."

One of the priests looks at the other, "Do you think she knows we're priests?"

"No it was a lucky guess. Let's wear some different clothes and come back tomorrow."

So the next day, they're sitting on the beach in different clothes, drinks in hand when here comes this same girl, and this time she has her top on. She passes by and says, "Good afternoon, Father, good afternoon Father." She walks on.

Then one of the priests jumps up. "Hey wait a minute, how did you know that we're priests?" She says, "Oh, I'm Sister Ruth from the church."

Joy and I had a lot of fun flying. We tried our best not to get caught having fun, but one day we were flying from El Paso to Clovis and we put that Cessna 210 on a three-axis autopilot. Everything was great, you know. I knew the way, had flown it forty times or so. We were in the backseat and we were quite busy. Then Joy said, "Oh my God, look out the left window." I look out. There's an airplane right beside us. And he just went right along beside us. I said, "Oh boy, well, we already got started, might as well finish."

Another time we were flying to Hawaii on a chartered 747. Well, there's a whole bunch of people, like three hundred people using six or eight bathrooms, so there was a line to get in. To sort of save time, Joy and I went in together.

And we kind of got involved…It took a little bit longer than usual.

Joy adds: *Let me just say, that when I married Jack he had a thirty-one and a half inch waist, all muscle, and he lifted weights until he was sixty-five years old. Incredible! He fit very nicely in that bathroom with me.*

There were people standing in line to get in the bathroom and when we opened the door, the two of us walked out, and everybody started clapping.

When I was down, I knew that I needed a strong system of beliefs to get back up. As Earl Nightingale says, "You don't get beat if you get knocked down, you only get beat if you stay down."

PART VI

Fairness

"As ye sow, so shall ye reap." It is the universal law of cause and effect. Our rewards in life will always match our service. If we want more rewards, we must first increase our service.

Twenty-eight

Down by the Rio Grande

I HAD STARTED Colonial Realty in 1974 but I didn't ever push that one too hard. We didn't have any residential salespeople to speak of. And then came the opportunity for a relationship with people in El Paso: Charlie Crowder, Lee Trevino, Don Whittington, and Jesse Whittenton.

I was in our office one morning and got this phone call from a fellow who identified himself as Charlie Crowder and he said, "I understand you guys have a golf course subdivision in Clovis." And I said, "Well, yes, we like to think that." We both laughed. And he said, "I wonder if I could see it sometime."

"Sure, sometime when you're in the vicinity of Clovis, I'd be glad to meet with you and show you around."

"Well, could I do that today?"

I guess so, when would you like to do it?"

Let's see, how about in an hour or an hour and fifteen minutes."

"How can you do that? Are you in town?"

"No, I'm in Albuquerque."

"How do you expect to get here in an hour and fifteen minutes?"

"Well, in my MU-2 jet prop airplane. I'd like to fly over there for you to show me what you guys do."

Having an interest in flying, I was most anxious to see this aircraft. I was sitting at the airport when the MU-2 landed. It was a Japanese-made jet prop airplane and it moved pretty fast, about 350 to four hundred miles per hour. Charlie made the entire flight in forty minutes from Albuquerque, 220 miles. First the pilot got off, I thought that was Charlie. He was kind of impressive looking so I ran up and said, "Mr. Crowder, I'm Jack Winton." And he said, "No, no. That's Mr. Crowder getting off the plane now."

As it turned out, Charlie Crowder was a promoter and a land trader with no experience in building homes or promoting homes but he knew what he wanted to do. He was a land swapper, some would've described him in other ways. But he was a personal acquaintance of Lyndon B. Johnson while he was president. Somehow, Charlie was able to get control of desirable federal-owned land by swapping it for other parcels that did not fit his program as well. Charlie was a big contributor to everybody; just in case the Republicans didn't win he would contribute the same amount to the Democrats, so whoever won, he was in. He was a wheeler-dealer back in those days.

> *One of Dr. Hill's patients had serious problems. So, Dr. Hill said, "I'm gonna give you six months to live." And, then he gave the patient his bill. The guy looks at the bill and says, "Good gosh. I can't ever pay this bill off in six months. What are you gonna do about it?"*
>
> *Dr. Hill said, "I'll give you six more months."*

I took Charlie into Clovis, went to the club, looked it over a little bit, put him on a golf cart, drove him around our golf course and then Marty came in and we visited with him together. Charlie said, "I would like to show you guys something that I'm doing in El Paso."

And we said, "Well, some day when you're going down there we'd be glad to meet you."

"No, no. I mean right now. We'll get in my plane and we'll fly down to El Paso. I'll drop you back in Clovis whenever you want me to."

So we figured we'd give our front seat in hell just for a ride in that airplane so we got in and took off. We landed at what was then the old Sunland Park Airport. It was in New Mexico, near El Paso, adjacent to the race track, which today is also a casino operation. We were met with a limo, and in the limo was Donny Whittington, the president of Lee Trevino Enterprises, Charlie's partner in the project. That afternoon we went to the Lancer's Club, high atop what was then the Coronado Bank Tower on Mesa Street on the west side of El Paso. Charlie went over to a window and said, "You see where all that work is going on way over there? Well, that's Santa Teresa, that's what I wanted you to see."

So we ate lunch and we drove over to where Charlie had pointed and took a look at Santa Teresa. They already had an eighteen-hole golf course that was barely developed, and another eighteen-hole golf course was under construction. We began a negotiation which lasted a good couple of months and it involved Jim Hart, a local tax attorney in Clovis. We had Jim when we needed him and ultimately we made a contract with Charlie Crowder, C. L. Crowder Investment Company. His company owned and controlled about twenty-five thousand acres of land there. He had grandiose ideas, and we didn't realize it at the time but he had probably tried everybody who was anybody in land development and promotion and finally got down to us.

> *A guy was called to an urgent meeting. When he got down there he couldn't find a parking space. He circled around and circled around and time was getting away from him and he thought, "This is such an important meeting. I cannot be any later than I already am."*
>
> *Finally he says, "God, if you will just find me a parking space, I will never drink anymore tequila as long as I live.*

I will go to Mass every Sunday. I will be a whole different person."

Right in front of him there, a car backs out, opening up a parking space. And as he's pulling into it he says, "Never mind God, I found one."

When we made the deal, it became necessary that either Marty or I move to El Paso and take over development activities and operations there. But neither of us wanted to leave Clovis, so we flipped a coin to see who would have to leave and go to El Paso. I lost the coin toss. So in October of 1975 Joy and I and the two girls moved to El Paso. That began a whole new chapter in our lives. We have been here for thirty-seven years.

A FLIP OF A COIN *can change your life
…and it did.*

Twenty-nine

New Partners

CHARLIE CROWDER was a wheeler-dealer. He was also a happy individual who would always have a joke for almost any occasion, perhaps that's where I picked up some of that. But when a deal came down—or as he would put it, "down to the nut cutting"—he would spout off and tell the story about Mrs. Jones and the dentist.

> *Mrs. Jones goes to the dentist and sits down in the chair The doctor comes in and starts to work on her. Suddenly he steps back a little ways and says, "Excuse me Mrs. Jones but I believe you have a hold of my testicles."*
>
> *And she says, "That's right, Doctor. Now we're not going to hurt each other are we?"*

That was Charlie's deal-making strategy. "We've got to make a deal that works for everybody and nobody gets hurt in the transaction."

Charlie Crowder had some pretty funny expressions. We'd be in a pretty important meeting with bankers or lawyers and he'd look up when somebody said something he liked, and he'd say, "If that's not a square deal, I'll kiss your ass."

Charlie was a smart individual with a lot of foresight. The land he had acquired for Santa Teresa was part of the Gadsden Purchase and the chain of title went from the Republic of Mexico to the United States government to Charlie Crowder. One of the first things he did once he owned the property was drill thirty-seven water wells, to prove there was water under that sand. And there was, lots of it. I always suspected that if the lawsuit between El Paso and the state of New Mexico (for exporting New Mexico water to Texas) had gone in El Paso's favor, Charlie would have started selling water instead of land.

So I spent about a year, ten to twelve hours a day, with Charlie Crowder, and that's where I tell people I got my Ph.D. in land development and dealings. He was really something.

He had met the Trevino group during his association with the land development around the Horizon Golf Club. Lee Trevino was an international golf celebrity and sportsman who had gotten his initial backing to go on the professional golf circuit from Donny Whittington and his cousin Jesse Whittenton. Their investment certainly paid off because Lee became a world class golfer and won a lot of tournaments. He was even *Sports Illustrated*'s Sportsman of the Year in 1971. Lee was also a great guy with a great sense of humor. There is this story about Lee: He was outside painting his house one day and a couple driving by stopped to ask how much he charged to paint houses. He said he didn't charge anything, but he got to sleep with the lady of the house. Jesse, Donny and Lee eventually formed a corporation called Lee Trevino Enterprises. It had investments in real estate and a few small businesses. They became partners with Charlie Crowder in the golf course and country club at Santa Teresa.

Lee was on the professional golf tour and not available in town very often. He would have to arrive at his tournament early, familiarize himself with the course, usually by walking it, and then practice. Then he'd be expected to play in the pro-am on a Wednesday with all the local celebrities. On Thursday, the PGA tournament began in earnest and he'd play Friday and Saturday, finishing up on Sunday.

But when Lee was off he'd come to town and stay for a week or so. We all celebrated and we invariably got together at Jesse's house or at somebody's residence. We would drink adult beverages and tell stories and Lee wound up generally sitting on a hassock out in the middle of a living room or a family room with a drink in his hand telling funny stories of things that happened to him out on the golf course on the pro tour. At that time, he was winning golf tournaments almost every week. At that time, first prize was typically forty thousand dollars, which is almost nothing by today's tournament standards.

Donny Whittington was the president of Lee Trevino Enterprises and he ran the operations of their organization. He was the business man of their group. Donny and I never got close, but his cousin Jesse and I became good friends.

Jesse Whittenton was a fabulous—and I really mean fabulous—football player. He was a high school All-American football player and was offered scholarships to play at universities all over the United States. I heard he was offered forty scholarships, but he elected, of all things, to live at home and play at what was then called Texas Western College, now the University of Texas at El Paso (UTEP). During his quarterbacking of his team in college, they set records that have never been equaled since. The guy was funny and was built like a superman. Upon graduation, he was drafted by the Los Angeles Rams in the NFL draft, and he played there for two seasons. He then joined the Green Bay Packers one year before Vince Lombardi became coach and he played for another five years under Lombardi. Jesse made the Pro Bowl twice, in 1961 and 1963, and he was a member of the Packers' 1961 and 1962 NFL Championship teams. He was inducted into the Packers Hall of Fame in 1976. Joy and I have always enjoyed traveling, so we took a trip to Green Bay Wisconsin to see the Green Bay Packers Hall of Fame, and there's a whole section of it dedicated to Jesse Whittenton.

Jesse had stories. He said that Vince Lombardi treated all the players the same: shitty. Jesse told that, at the first meeting of every football season, Vince Lombardi would walk up and down in front of the assembled team with a football in his hand. And when he finally got ready to speak, he would say, "Gentlemen. This is a football and when I'm through with you, you will know everything there is to know about a football."

While Jesse was playing in Green Bay, Donny, his cousin, moved out there and they opened a Mexican restaurant patterned after Leo's Mexican Food in El Paso. They had a very successful restaurant there largely because of Jesse's association with it. He would often be there eating and people would come by to see him because he was one of the main stars on the Green Bay Packers football team.

It was an exciting time and we felt very fortunate to be associated with this group. We created the Santa Teresa Development Corporation, the entity that would be developing the land and selling the lots. Charlie's contribution was to provide us land. Lee Trevino's company and Charlie's company owned half of the corporation and Marty and I owned the other half. It was a rather long multi-page contract that spelled out the details and responsibilities. We never owned the land other than as Charlie fronted the development company the parcels for development as we needed them. Charlie didn't get paid anything for the land until we sold lots. We put the land in at a fair and reasonable price.

It really is easier to win because ninety-five percent of the population is not trying to get to where you want to be.

Thirty

Santa Teresa

We couldn't find a place to live in El Paso. But there was a place called Lee Trevino Apartments, on north Mesa Street that the Trevino group owned. They were one thousand square feet, two-bedroom, two-bathroom apartments. There was a living room, a kitchen and a dining area, all in a nice arrangement. We had them put a doorway between two of the apartments, so Joy and I and the girls lived there for about a year with four bedrooms, four bathrooms, two kitchens and two living areas. It was on the west side of El Paso not too far from Country Club Road, which led to the Santa Teresa development.

Charlie and I were together constantly. His wife was still living in Albuquerque and Charlie had a place at the Trevino apartments. Joy usually made supper and Charlie ate with us occasionally in the apartment.

When we began the actual development, Santa Teresa consisted of a dirt road that ran from the dead end of Country Club Road to the golf courses. The pro shop and snack bar were a couple of portable trailers. The club house, the pro shop, the swimming pool, and the tennis courts were all under construction. Lee's, Donny's and Jesse's homes were also all under construction.

So we picked out certain areas we knew would need some golf course development with upscale homes. We also knew we would need some medium range housing and an area for condos. We laid out what we were going to do and where. We had a full-time engineer that Charlie had already hired who was available to us and an AIA architect who was on Charlie's staff that I had access to. Charlie made it clear to them all that I was their new partner and their new boss and, "Whatever he says to do, you do."

I officed with these guys in the Lee Trevino Apartments until we got an office building built out at the development. The engineer, Ron King, is still around. He was a bright young fellow who had graduated from New Mexico State with his degree in civil engineering. He did all of the engineering for the development and he and I went to meetings at the county planning department and made presentations. He was always slower than I wanted him to be and he'd say, "Well you're just in too big a hurry."

Within a year we had several developments of various kinds available to build homes in Santa Teresa. Joy and I chose a lot on the golf course and built our first home there. I started attending meetings of the El Paso Association of Homebuilders. They recognized people who were likely to contribute something, so they put me on their board of directors right away. Our new home was in the 1976 Home Builders Home Show. Back then it was a scattered-site home show with a map showing people where the homes were. We had completely furnished our home but we didn't move into it until after the show.

I recall that in a builder's association board meeting after the '76 show I proposed we have the next show in Santa Teresa. One of the members, a homebuilder named Joe Hanson, was kind of a big dog. He was a big old burly guy and he stood up and said, "Now let me see if I have this right. He wants to have the El Paso Association of Homebuilders

Home Show not in El Paso but in something called Santa Teresa that doesn't really exist yet in a completely different state. Does that make any sense to you guys?"

Eventually though, we had the show in Santa Teresa. Lee Trevino, through Donny Whittington, had an ability to get news coverage and so he would simply call a press conference about anytime he wanted to. I would go with him and tell people what we were thinking about. It was the biggest home show ever with over twenty-one thousand people coming through the homes.

There was a lot of excitement and high expectations for Santa Teresa in the entire region. The club membership was growing exponentially and we were selling lots. We had five or six builders from El Paso including Don Wiley, George Henthorne, and Jim Reid. We were able to get a few builders from Las Cruces. Commodore Hines and his sons all built houses there and so did Mickey Clute. We also had some builders from Clovis build some homes. More importantly though, people were buying the homes and they were moving into Santa Teresa. I was building and so was Marty. I did the Paseo Village section, modeled after the one we had done in Clovis. Marty was building quads. We were both building garden homes on the golf course.

One of my stories that I used to tell Realtors was that in a town of twenty thousand people, a golf course subdivision should not survive, should not be successful. Marty Shaeffer and I didn't know that you couldn't make that thing work in Clovis, but we did make it work. Today there's over 1,400 families living on those 640 acres that we set out to develop in the early 1970s. And now, we had Santa Teresa moving in that same direction.

I came into the office one morning and Ron King said, "Oh boy, you won't believe it but I got a call from the Thompsons who said the neighbor's dog got into the trash can and tore it up and she's mad as hell. I got a call from the Whartons who said the kids next door threw a rock through their window and he said, 'What are we going to do about it?'"

I said, "Ron, if we can't figure out some way of keeping people from moving into this subdivision, they are going to ruin it."

We had a lot of fun doing the Santa Teresa deal. There is nothing like taking a blank piece of property and turning it into a place where people love to live.

A Realtor called me one time asking if we would rent our house. I explained that it was for sale, not rent. Every house I have ever lived in as an adult has been for sale at some price. He told me he was looking for a place that a Hollywood studio could use to house an actor while filming in El Paso. He told me what they would pay and since it was over four times what our house payment was at the time, I quickly agreed. Our first "tenant" was Robert Blake. He was in town filming a movie that was never released called *The Hamster of Happiness*. I am not sure why it wasn't released because at that time Blake had a hit TV show called *Baretta*, and the movie was directed by a big name director, Hal Ashby, who also stayed at Santa Teresa while they filmed the movie.

We rented our house with everything in it—furniture, sheets, towels, silverware, everything someone living there would need. We took our clothes and personal items and left everything else for two or three months while they lived there. The studio paid everything. We spent the summer in Ruidoso and I commuted daily in my plane back to El Paso.

A year later, Hollywood called again and asked if we could let Jack Nicholson stay in our home while he was in El Paso filming a movie called *The Border*. I told them I would, but I doubled the price that had been paid previously. Surprisingly, they agreed. While Nicholson was in El Paso, they had a big event for him at the Sun Bowl and he was given a brand new Harley-Davidson motorcycle to commemorate the movie *Easy Rider*. He drove it from the Sun Bowl and parked it in our living room, never moving it, until he went back to California. Fortunately it was brand new, so there was no oil leak. When we got the house back, we discovered a script for *The Postman Always Rings Twice* that he had left in the closet and a freezer full of high quality steaks.

The logo for the country club was a Mexican sombrero and Lee had a specially-built golf cart which I used to take dignitaries around all week long, and its top was a big sombrero. They kept it charged up all the time and whenever bankers or title company dignitaries or county people came to town, I would drive them over to the barn and get Lee's cart and take them around and show them everything.

Within a little less than two years, Santa Teresa had grown to a small community of about three hundred households.

Aerodynamically,
the bumble bee shouldn't be able to fly,
but the bumble bee doesn't know it
so it goes on flying anyway.

—Mary Kay Ash

Thirty-one

The Deal Falls Apart

At one point along the way Charlie Crowder decided he did not want to share his twenty-five thousand-acre sandbox. He began a process of buying all of us out. I never really understood what the dynamics were for Charlie at the time, but his intent was to be in it alone. And that's what he got.

It had been less than two years. I was living in a big house on the golf course but Marty wanted me to move back to Clovis. I didn't want to. You look at Clovis and you're looking at a max market of maybe one hundred new homes built per year. Down here in El Paso, with 700,000 people, we were looking at three or four thousand homes being built in a year. So I didn't want to go back and he finally said, "Well, if you're not going to come back, let's sit down and negotiate a deal for you to sell the Clovis stuff to me." That's what we did.

Marty made me a great offer and he borrowed part of it from the Citizen's Bank. What wasn't available in the companies that we had, he paid in cash. That was about 1978 and so I began, as best I could, to become a wheeler-dealer in El Paso.

Joy and me, 1982.

We still say that Marty and I were the only people in the last thirty-five years that made any money from Santa Teresa and there's probably a certain amount of truth to that. When we were there, we had it moving, and we were gaining even more momentum. There was a variety of home sizes and prices including condos, patio homes and single family homes. In that short period of time, almost three hundred homes were built. It is a shame to see that the place has never made a movement towards its potential.

Lee Trevino still has a very bad taste in his mouth about the El Paso thing. Joy and I were in Los Cabos, Mexico one time when Lee happened to be staying at the same resort. He was playing in the skins game. Lee was sitting in a station wagon in front, while his driver and his factotum man had gone in to register them and get the key. Joy and I were coming back from playing tennis. So we go over, knock on the window of the car and he rolls the window down. He wasn't the same old friendly guy, but he was polite and cordial. That was the last time I saw him, other than when he was on TV.

I kept a relationship with Jesse longer than anybody from that group. He and his wife Peggy used to play tennis with Joy and I. And Jesse and I would take on the girls and Jesse would say, "I'm going to play the net if you're serving, and if you can, just stay out of my way." It seemed to me that Jesse could leap straight up in the air about twelve feet. If a ball was coming over—*bingo!*—Jesse'd go up in the air and smash it. He'd never played tennis before in his life and he was fantastic.

Jesse and Peggy ended up divorcing, but Joy has maintained a close friendship with Peggy over all of these years. They talk, or text message, almost daily. Peggy remarried nearly twenty years ago to a great guy named Al Domasin. Al is one of those rare individuals who can talk to anyone about almost any subject. He is a wine connoisseur, plays polo and looks like a model from *GQ Magazine*, always dressed immaculately and perfectly matched. He is a lot of fun and we have gone on many vacations with them. We also go visit them regularly at their home in Newport Beach, California.

I am not sure about any of the details of the Trevino group's buyout, but one of the moves Charlie made was to trade for my and Marty's interest in Santa Teresa by deeding us a large piece of land on top of a mountain in Ruidoso, New Mexico. The chain of title went from the federal government to Charlie Crowder to me and Marty. Also in the trade were all the lots that he had developed in a subdivision called Black Forest, a mountain subdivision in Ruidoso. The Black Forest subdivision had been a piece of land that Charlie had in the mountains that he had subdivided into residential building sites. He even set up an office in town to sell lots, and he had sold quite a few. But he still had seventy or eighty lots, so he traded us all of those plus the 160-acre parcel of land up on the side and the top of a mountain.

I used to go up there occasionally. I ruined a good Cadillac taking it up a road that a Sherman tank couldn't have climbed. Once I knocked off the oil pan. I used to like to walk all over the property. Where the trees were thinned out sufficiently, it was almost like looking out at the whole world.

In the process of closing out our Colonial Park development, Marty and I sat and worked for three days and we came to an agreement on a value for every lot and every acre of all our joint properties, including the club and everything in Clovis. In the end he gave me his interest in the Ruidoso property plus cash. Except for ownership in an airplane, Marty and I did not have a business relationship for a few years. But we each felt we'd been treated fairly in all of our dealings and in the termination of them.

Don't waste time talking about your problems with people who can't solve them. Don't talk about your health unless it's good or you're talking to your doctor. It won't help you. It can't help others.

—EARL NIGHTINGALE

Thirty-two

Up in the Air

With no more partnerships, I was in a position to call my own shots and not have to answer to anyone. One of the things I decided was to diversify and build houses in a lot of different cities, so that if the market cratered in one city, it might not be so bad in another city.

This was in 1978, so I had been flying for sixteen years. But this new direction was going to give me a chance to log more flying hours than I ever imagined. I was building houses in Hobbs, Carlsbad, Clovis, Roswell, Farmington and Ruidoso, and I made that route about once a week in a Cessna 210. Sometimes I would carry tools, sledge hammers or even bags of concrete. I even took a concrete crew from El Paso to Farmington once. As a result, I have logged more hours as a pilot than most people with twenty-five years in the Air Force. In my twenty-three year flying career, I logged 4,300 hours.

Marty and I had bought a Cessna 210 and we always managed to write off an airplane. If I was building in Albuquerque and Tucumcari, there was a reason for me to have a plane, but Marty got more flying in than I did. He eventually got an instrument rating. I only had a private pilot's

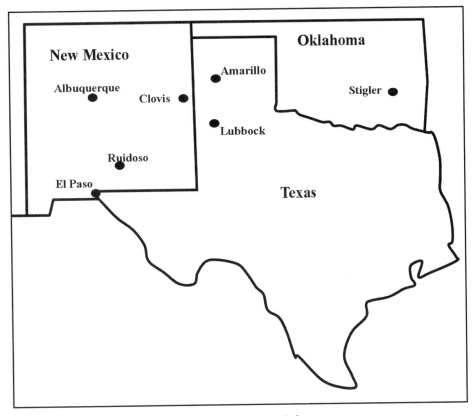

The three-state area where I have spent my life.

rating which I got when I had about three hundred hours logged. We eventually owned two Cessna 210s, one with struts on the wings. Then we got rid of that airplane and bought an upgraded Cessna 210, where they had eliminated the struts on the wings and kicked the horsepower up ten or twenty percent which made it go a lot faster. When we bought the brand new one, I kept the old one in El Paso with me, Marty kept the new one in Clovis with him and then we'd change airplanes every once in a while. I'd keep the new one for a month or two or three and he'd keep the old one and then we'd change back.

I had some narrow escapes as a pilot. When I had had my license for about six years, two of our sons were visiting my parents in Oklahoma. My dad had been telling me that there was a farmer nearby, just a mile or so from the house who had a couple of airplanes and a dirt landing strip out there. Since I needed to go get the boys, and our plane wasn't available for some reason, I called an Air Force buddy of mine. I had sold houses to some of the people stationed at Cannon Air Force Base just outside of Clovis, and one guy had become a special friend of mine. He told me that he had a private pilot's license and he would like to help me out. So I said, "I'll pay the rent on a plane if you'll fly me to Oklahoma to pick up my kids because I'm not checked out in that plane." We went out to the airport and the owner of the plane said, "I am sorry but I don't know you," to my friend. So my friend said, "Why don't you give me a check ride?" So they did a little circle and he came back and said, "Okay, he's okay."

We flew it down to Oklahoma, circled the house a couple of times, and I spotted the dirt strip and said, "There it is."

He said, "Okay, I think I see it."

It was a hot, hot one hundred-plus degree day in Oklahoma, and he tried to bring the plane in. On a hot day, heat rises from the ground. Those waves of heat cause lift on the plane and make it hard to touch down. So this plane just floated and floated and floated, and he took off and circled around again. He said, "Okay, this time I'm gonna make it." And he almost did. We went around again and were doing pretty well until he saw that it actually was not going to work, and then he tried to take off again. At the end of this little dirt strip was a three or four strand barbwire fence, and it caught the wheels of the airplane as we flew over it, and we had a little bit of a tumble there. Didn't hurt anybody.

And that's the only actual wreck I was ever in, but I had some other interesting experiences.

> *On a transatlantic flight, the pilot announces that there is a problem with the plane and that they need to lose some weight. So the crew start throwing the luggage out. The pilot comes on again and says they need to lose even more weight. So they start throwing the seats out and it is*

The rental plane we crashed in Oklahoma—the only actual wreck I was ever in. The plane tripped over the top strand of a barbwire fence at the end of a little dirt landing strip.

> *still not light enough. So some people volunteer to jump. A Frenchman says, "Viva la France," and jumps out. A British guy says, "Long live the Queen," and he jumps out. A Texan jumps up and says, "Remember the Alamo," and throws out two Mexicans.*

Another time when I was married to Lunell, I flew her and the kids to Oklahoma. On the day we were supposed to leave to go back to Clovis there was storm weather building to the west. I thought we could make it by either going around it or over it. So we went ahead and took off. Once we were in the air, it became apparent we could not go over the storm because it was just too tall. So I started to go around it by heading south. The storm kept building and I kept skirting it until we were almost out of gas and we were also off of our map. I was finally able to find a place to land, and discovered it was Bonham, Texas. We were able to get some gas and a highway map to help us find our way home. I think that was Lunell's last trip in a plane I was piloting.

> *The airline pilot came on the loudspeaker and says, "Ladies and gentlemen. This is your captain speaking. I have some good news for you and I have some bad news for you. First the bad news: we are lost. Next the good news: we are making damn good time."*

I was flying alone one time and suddenly the windshield became covered with oil. That will make you pucker a little bit. I knew where the airport was, and it wasn't too far away, and looking out the side I managed to bring the old Tri-Pacer in alright. An oil seal had broken and there wasn't anything serious, but there could have been.

Joy and I had some fun flying experiences. One day the weather report was not good. It wasn't that bad either but by the time we flew to Clovis from El Paso, the wind had kicked up to about eighty miles per hour. However, it was pretty much straight down the runway. I didn't know what else to do so I asked on the radio, "How many people do you have around there?"

"Well, there's four or five people standing around here waiting for the weather to clear."

I said, "Well I'll tell you what I'm going to do. I'm going to land the plane, but the wind is blowing just about as hard as the landing speed for the plane, so when I get it up close enough to the building, tell everyone inside to run out and grab onto the struts and hang onto the plane so it won't blow away."

And, that's what we did. Pilots would always stick together and help

Joy's dad, Dub Chumley, helped me navigate along the Lubbock highway.

each other out of trouble. I had to travel 130 miles per hour to make fifty miles per hour but the touchdown speed for the plane was about eighty. Once I got it down, the wind continued to blow, but I gave it a little extra power and ran it over to the building and then sure enough, the guys came running out and they grabbed the wing struts of the plane. With six or eight hundred pounds of additional weight I was able to shut off the plane and get it tied down.

I usually flew VFR, Visual Flight Rules as opposed to IFR, Instrument Flight Rules. I said IFR means I Follow Roads because sometimes coming from Oklahoma the weather would be so bad that I'd find a highway that I was familiar with and we'd just fly five or six hundred feet above it.

On one trip to Oklahoma, when I found out where we were, I looked at the map and realized that the mountains were higher than we were. So I'll say we did some quick climbing. Mr. Chumley, Joy's daddy, was sitting in the front seat by me for his first plane ride ever. I didn't know where we were or where we were headed, but when we cleared the clouds, Mr. Chumley, who was a truck driver, said, "Look, I think that's the old road to Lubbock." I followed that road and we made it home. Thank goodness he recognized where we were.

As a pilot, you decide your destination and the route you will take. Even though you cannot see your destination, you know that if you take off, stay on a certain heading, you will get to where you expected to go. Goal setting is deciding where you want to go and a lot like piloting a plane.

PART VII

Humility

Humility is no substitute for a good personality.

Thirty-three

Blowin' and Goin'

After the Santa Teresa deal fell apart and Marty and I had divided our interests, I decided to stay in El Paso. I still owned some lots in Paseo Village in Santa Teresa, and I had a model home there, so I moved my offices into the model and we continued to build those patio homes. I was also building in Hobbs, Carlsbad, Clovis, Roswell, Farmington and Ruidoso.

There was a subdivision called La Paz Estates and it hadn't really taken off too dramatically. It was financed by El Paso Federal Savings and Loan, headed by Bob Payne, whom I had gone hunting with for Sandhill Cranes. He called me and said, "If you will build these homes we will give you interim financing to do it with." They were also the people who were handling bond money that was available in the state of Texas at the then unheard of low price of nine and a quarter percent interest for permanent mortgages. That was when interest rates were going at twelve and thirteen percent and they said, "Maybe we can bundle enough of the funds that will be needed to handle your deals."

And so we took that on. There were 229 lots in the La Paz Estates subdivision and though several homes had already been built and a few more were built later, we built 179 of those homes. We took down one lot, built a model home, furnished it and used it for an office. That project lasted for two or three years.

When people found out that my buyers were getting a disproportionate share of the nine and a quarter percent money, threats of lawsuits and all kinds of things like that took place. In fact, I had one guy tell me, "If you don't get me a nine and a quarter percent loan I'm going to sue you and take everything you have." Which wasn't a helluva lot back then, but can you imagine today getting so excited about getting a loan for nine and a quarter percent when mortgages are now going for around four percent?

This was around the time when I first got to know Bill Hagan, who worked for Bob Payne. I had met Bill when he was working for Valley Savings out of Artesia, New Mexico, but he soon went to work at El Paso Federal. We became good friends. Bill is a sharp individual. He grew up in Lovington, graduated from ENMU in Portales, and moved to El Paso, where he became a mover and shaker. He is behind the scenes, but Bill stays on top of things. He always knows what is going on. He has brought us lots of opportunities and has always treated us fairly. I have always admired the work he does with the Boy Scouts of America. He is one of the founders of Rocky Mountain Mortgage and we do a lot of business with them.

Bill brought us another development when La Paz was winding down: Western Skies Patio Homes. Some builders had put this whole thing together and then couldn't make it fly. So we moved into Western Skies and started building these four-unit, two-story condo buildings. We took one of the buildings for our offices. It felt like the big time.

Herschel Stringfield was our chief superintendent at that time. He has been one of the best individuals I have ever worked with. He went to high school in Alamogordo, New Mexico, then went to work for a homebuilder while studying engineering in college. That builder built one home at a time, then sold it. His own crew did everything. They dug the footings, they poured the concrete, they did everything except electrical and plumbing. And so Herschel learned to do the work of almost every trade required to build a home. He would pour the concrete for the slab, and he would frame the houses, roof the houses. He would also sheetrock them. He thoroughly learned the business that way.

Herschel subsequently moved to El Paso with his wife Debbie and went to work for a very successful builder named John Schatzman. And that's where Herschel became a friend of John Livingston who was a friend and a backer of Schatzman. I had hired a young man named Bruce Blaine, who had a degree in construction management from ENMU. Bruce was a sharp, eager-beaver young fellow and Bruce hired Herschel as a superintendent for us. Herschel was obviously head and shoulders above anybody we had had in that position before.

We had acquired some lots in Mesa Hills, through Bill Hagan, and we were building homes there. These were nice lots with fantastic views. We turned it over to Herschel and we'd go out and walk the houses with him. He'd take a notebook and make notes on everything.

Joy and I took a special interest in those homes because of their size and quality. We built ourselves a six thousand square foot house on two lots with unobstructed views. That is where we were living when that house was eventually foreclosed. It was 606 Skydale and we lived there for eight years.

Bruce wanted to be closer to his hometown of Raton, New Mexico, so we decided to form a company and build homes in Albuquerque. We formed a company called Winton and Blaine, Inc. I said to Bruce, "Obviously you've been running things here in El Paso, so you have to replace yourself." And he said, "Well the only real choice is Herschel Stringfield. This guy is fantastic."

What Jesus said to the disciples at The Last Supper:
"If you guys want to get in the picture
you have to get on this side of the table."

We were also building homes in Black Forest in Ruidoso on the lots we acquired from Charlie Crowder. I also planned on developing the mountain land that we had gotten from him. I went so far as to have it engineered and made presentations to the county officials. In fact I went with the engineer to a night meeting and he made a pretty good representation. It seemed like all the townspeople showed up for it that evening in Carrizozo, the county seat for Lincoln County. The engineer was making the presentation and one man said, "Who is the guy with you?"

He said, "He's the landowner."

"Well, we're not used to that, usually the landowner doesn't have enough interest in it to show up. We're impressed so let's talk to him."

They approved our development.

That was in the early 1980s. We never did develop it. The impending train wreck was already in progress.

Honesty, unfailing integrity, is good business. In fact, Mirabeau wrote that if honesty did not exist, someone should invent it as the best means of getting rich.

—Earl Nightingale

Thirty-four

Train Wreck

I N THE MID-1980S, we hit the wall. It wasn't just our companies. All the homebuilders in Texas, and the rest of the country, hit a wall. Later they called it the savings and loan crisis. The S&Ls were accepting one year CDs but making thirty year mortgages and it became evident that what they were having to pay for their money was much more than the interest on loans they had made.

Everyone I know blamed the savings and loan collapse on Paul Volcker, the Chairman of the United States Federal Reserve. His manipulation of things let the interest rate get so out of sight and literally cripple the national economy. If Paul Volcker had done things differently, this very well might not have happened. If he had kept interest rates at a lower level, business might have survived. Others have said it was the deregulation of the savings and loans, allowing them to be partners in deals they made loans on. But I don't really know the causes of the situation. I was just one of the people who got caught in the circumstances. As Walter Cronkite said, "And that's the way it is."

Joy and me, mid-1980s.

Almost all savings and loans went upside down, or in other words: bankrupt! I sometimes ask myself if there were things I would do differently. I might have been able to stretch it out because eventually the S&Ls became the RTC, the Resolution Trust Corporation. That's where all the assets of the failed savings and loans went. If I had stretched it out, I could have probably settled some of our home loans for thirty to fifty cents on the dollar, like most RTC deals went. But that is hindsight; it doesn't do any good to play "what if" with the past, other than to learn from it. That was a historical time for the U.S. economy. Some made a lot of money off RTC deals. Some didn't.

In 1985, we saw the handwriting on the wall and called a meeting of all the employees and explained to them that we were going to continue, but we would have to reduce the staff by at least fifty percent. We cut expenses to the bone, but still didn't make it.

In 1986 or 1987 we had many pre-sold homes with pre-approved buyers. Then the prime rate went to twenty percent and we had to borrow money at prime plus two. Mortgages topped out at seventeen percent and our buyers who had qualified at twelve or thirteen percent interest before we had started building their home were now having to get qualified at the higher rates. Most jumped out of the boat at fifteen percent, so we were stuck with all those homes that could not be sold.

I fed everything I had into paying interest on the construction loans until the money ran out. All I could do was keep writing checks to pay the interest on the loans that the company had made and that I had personally made. Eventually I ran out of money and I do mean out, completely. I didn't have enough money for Joy to buy a new pair of shoes.

During a crash, you know, "Hope springs eternal in the human breast." I always thought that the economy was going to straighten itself out. If I had realized that we were throwing money into a bottomless pit, I might have declared bankruptcy sooner and tried to salvage more assets, but it never really dawned on me that this was the way we were moving.

So we filed for personal and corporate bankruptcy in 1988. I was fifty-five years old.

> *Donald Duck and Daisy were sitting in the lobby of a hotel where they had registered, and they were holding hands. Donald got a little amorous and proposed to Daisy that, "Maybe this would be a good time for us to have a little action tonight."*
>
> *Daisy said, "Well, do you have any condoms with you?"*
> *"No, I don't."*
> *"Well, if you don't have any condoms, there won't be any action."*
> *So he says, "Okay. Hold on."*
> *He goes to the hotel desk and says to the desk clerk quietly, "Do you by chance sell condoms here?" And the clerk reaches in the drawer underneath and comes up with a package and lays 'em on the counter. He said, "Would you like for me to put these on your bill?"*
> *Donald Duck says, "Heck no, man. I'd suffocate."*

We had an awful lot of property foreclosed on in El Paso. I had used the land in Ruidoso as collateral for a loan, so we lost that land too.

The bank retired me from flying. They said, "Do you owe any money on that airplane?" and I said, "No." "Well, sell it and bring us the money." So I did and I haven't flown a plane since then.

Joy remembers: *We sold the Cadillac and bought a mini-van with fake wooden paneling on the sides. When I took Monica and Kristel to school, they would say "Mom, drop us off around the block," because they were so embarrassed.*

> *I have decided that I would rather be healthy and rich,*
> *than sickly and poor.*

We cut way back in our lifestyle and we both started selling real estate. Joy got a license and I had a broker's license in Texas and New Mexico. We joined a firm called the Future Company and started selling homes for them.

After we started doing real estate and got our feet wet, Joy was taking listings of large and expensive homes. She would hold open houses and meet people. Then she would call me in to help her with the closing of the sale. One month after the train wreck occurred, the total commissions from the sales of her listings and the buyers that she handled were in the mid five figures. Joy could really sell, if she wanted to. She could be one of the most amazing real estate salespersons ever. But she never really liked it.

I guess because of my positive upbeat nature, I was happy to be selling real estate. We made a positive contribution to the Future Company's

Me with my good friend Charles Nieman who helped me tremendously when I needed it.

business and we were looked up to in meetings that we attended.

This was also a period of time when I met Charles Nieman, the pastor at Abundant Living Faith Center. At that time, he held services in a rented warehouse on Missouri Street. He started his ministry in 1977 and has grown it to be one of the largest in the Southwest with approximately twenty thousand members. We became very close friends and I appreciated his presentation of Christianity and the nature of the New Testament God: The God of abundance, the unjudging God who lets us judge ourselves, the God of love who only wants us to love Him and each other as we should love ourselves, the God of creativity, who wanted me to co-create with Him.

Dr. Robert Schuller *said,*
"Tough Times Don't Last; Tough People Do."
We read that and we hung on to our beliefs.

Thirty-five

Back in the Saddle

Although we enjoyed selling real estate, it was hard on both Joy and myself. After having had such previous success, sometimes we felt that we were down and worthless and had no value. It was a very bad experience, but I knew somehow that things would get better, and they did.

There was an old boy who had been in the land business and the mobile home business named John Livingston. He came in with some capital and rescued Southwest Savings and Loan in El Paso. I had done some business with John on some land deals back at Santa Teresa, in the early days. He called me one day before we went bankrupt and he said, "I know what you're going through and I know Herschel. I've known Herschel for a long time when he was working for John Schatzman." And he said, "I want to invite you and Herschel to have lunch with me." So we went to a little greasy spoon called the Riviera Restaurant, which is still one of my favorites.

As we sat there, John said, "Now fellows, you know that Southwest Savings and Loan can't loan any money to an upside-down corporation.

And so I'm going to suggest that you just go ahead and get past the misery and declare Winton Homes, Inc. bankrupt and form a new company, and I'll figure out a way to loan enough money for you to build a couple of houses at a time, even though the new company won't have any assets." Well, that was a big help.

Herschel and I got together afterwards and I said, "Hersch, when you form a new company you've got to capitalize it. What can you come up with?"

He scratched his head and thought a little bit and he said, "Well maybe five hundred dollars."

And I said, "I think I can scrape up $1,500." So in 1988, we formed Winton & Associates with capital of two thousand dollars. We used financing from Southwest Savings on interim construction loans to get started building product again and we continued, let's say, to have a presence in the El Paso marketplace.

Rodger Lovrenich, who had lived next door to me in Santa Teresa, called one day and said, "I know what you do and I know how you do it, and I believe in it. And I believe in you and I've got a few dollars that I've saved for my future retirement, and it's not making me a very good return, so if you can show me how you can utilize my resources to our mutual advantage, I'll see what I can do." So I went back to him with a proposal.

I said, "We will borrow your funds as if you were a bank. We'll pay you a one percent origination fee and prime plus two for the use of that money. We will charge a fee of $1,500 to build each house. When a home sells and the net proceeds are available, we'll pay off your loan and split fifty-fifty all the money that is made on the deal."

We used Rodger's funds to build an upscale home in a home show on the east side of El Paso in 1989. It was the finest designed, furnished and decorated home in the show. Joy had gone to furniture stores and said, "I need you to loan me furniture for this show, and you can have all the

***Right**—Herschel Stringfield.*
***Below**—Joy and myself. These photos from the late 1980s were taken from the back of one of our early marketing magazines for Winton & Associates.*

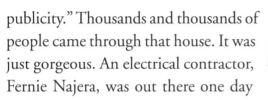

publicity." Thousands and thousands of people came through that house. It was just gorgeous. An electrical contractor, Fernie Najera, was out there one day and he said, "How's your house? Are you going to get it ready in time?"

"I think so," I said.

Fernie opened the front door and said, "This is the prettiest house I've ever seen."

This particular home had a circular foyer with pillars every so often, arches and a chandelier, all looking into a great room with a fireplace. It sold during the show and Rodger got his payback plus a rather substantial profit. So he got excited and said, "Let's keep doing this."

We concentrated on high-end, high-quality homes. And it caught on. We gave each home a name, such as "The Barcelona" or "The Vintage." Even to this day, we still have people that come in and say, "I remember that you had a home in a show nineteen years ago. That home has been in my mind all these years and now I'm ready for a new home and so I wonder if you can dust off that plan and build it for me."

We built homes using Rodger's funds again and again, because after those houses were finished, they sold well. He and I continued to become closer friends all the time, and we would meet for lunch every Thursday. He is a brilliant man. He had a wall displaying all the patents he had developed. He had gone to college at the General Motors Institute, and he worked for them for many years. During his tenure with GM he invented and had the first patent on the hydraulic backhoe, and he has the first metal model of it attached to a little Ford tractor.

I said, "How on earth did you come up with that?"

And he said, "Well, I studied hydraulics and I studied steam shovels. And I thought to myself that I don't see why that same thing can't be done with hydraulics instead of cables and pulleys." So he built a little scale model and found out sure enough it did work, and he got the patent on it.

"That must have made you billions of dollars."

"No; it made General Motors billions of dollars. Since I worked for them at the time of the invention, they owned it."

Great guy. I don't see him enough.

About the time Rodger and I were working together, we would meet at Pancho's Mexican Buffet every Thursday. That is where I met Patricia Cruz. She was working at Pancho's as a waitress and always gave us great service for our three- or four-hour meetings. After a few months of this, I asked her if she planned on being a waitress all her life. She said, "No, as a matter of fact, this is my last week here." I asked her if she had another job lined up, and she said no but she was going to be

"The Barcelona"

looking for an office job. So I asked her to give me a call. The next day, I was sitting at my desk and was told, "Somebody named Patricia Cruz is here to see you." I said, "Okay," and the most gorgeous creature you've ever seen came in with a light purple dress, kind of low cut. I said, "My god, who are you?"

"You said to come see you about a job." Then it dawned on me that she was the waitress from Pancho's.

She started as a receptionist and ended as a right hand assistant to me. She ran the office, did land development work with the engineers, worked with the city, worked with everybody. She met and married the manager of Ferguson Supply while working at our office. Ram Saenz was a top notch producer and after his marriage to Patricia, he was promoted to a high level position in San Antonio where he took over a multimillion dollar company.

You will find that at odd moments, when you least expect it, really great ideas will begin to bubble up from your subconscious. When they do, write them down as soon as you can. Just one great idea can completely revolutionize your work and, as a result, your life!

—Earl Nightingale

Thirty-six

God, Please Give Me Another Boom
(and I Promise Not to Blow it)

As business improved we had the chance to have fun again, and we were able to mix fun with business. On Valentine's Day 1990, we met the Shaeffers in Las Vegas. The girls were shopping and Marty and I were sitting in the lobby in a comfortable booth watching people go by, and Marty said, "Well tell me what exciting things are you looking at?"

I told him about a piece of land that Charlie Crowder had lost to the bank in foreclosure that was bought by a real estate man named Bob Karch, of BKB Properties. I'd been trying to get him to develop it into lots because we needed the lots and felt there was a market there. I'd called him every day and every day he told me to stop calling him. Finally, I said to myself, "I'm going to give him one last call."

He got on the line and I asked, "Have you decided yet to develop that land?"

"No, dammit and I'm getting tired of you calling me about it."

I am a pretty stubborn fellow, so I asked him, "Is there any way I can get you to develop it or sell it to me?"

"Hell yes, I'll sell it to you."

This was an absolute shock. I said, "What would you have to get for it? If I can afford it, I'd like to buy it from you."

"I'd like exactly what I have in it, and I bought it from the bank after it had been foreclosed on from Charlie Crowder."

"How much is that?"

"Just exactly what I paid plus the taxes I put into it."

"Do you know how much that is?"

"Just come down to my office and I'll pull out the file and show it to you."

So I said, "I'll be over at your office in five minutes."

So I went down there and—*bingo!*—there it was, we agreed on a price. The property had already been planned, platted and recorded for close to fifteen years from back when Ron King and I originally platted this land during our Santa Teresa days!

Marty by now was in the aviation business in Santa Fe with a man named Herb Marchman. He asked while we were in Las Vegas, "How are you fixed for cash to pull this off?"

"Well, it's going to drain me. I'm gonna have to rake up the cash to get the financing to buy the land and start the development of it."

And he said, "Well, do you want a partner in that?"

"I don't know. What do you have in mind?"

"Herb and I, we've had some pretty good success. What if we provide the cash that you need, and we own one third and you own two thirds of this?"

We set up our original land development deal and it was called Sunnyview LLC, and later we added Viewpoint Acreage, LLC. We got Jim Hart to do the paperwork for the formation of the company, the operating agreement, etc. I was to be the manager of the LLC. Marty and Herb never did have to sign a note, so I had all the liability. They put up the money through Santa Fe Jet, the aviation company

Me and Marty Shaeffer, Santa Fe, summer, 1988—enjoying one of our business/pleasure trips.

they owned. We hit a major home run with Sunnyview and Viewpoint. We were able to move on it quickly and we developed it one street at a time. The land development costs were reasonable, and we were selling lots at a very good price. That got us restarted in the land development business in El Paso.

Then another opportunity came along. An investor named Chris Cummings had developed a subdivision called River Run in El Paso, but he wasn't a builder, and the builders that he had contracted to produce homes weren't that successful at marketing, so he was not too pleased. He contacted me and said, "Would you like to buy this development from me?" I said, "Well, I don't know, it depends on a lot of things."

Herb and Marty wanted to be in on that too, so we formed River Run LLC, and we bought the subdivision. We made the deal on Monday

One of our upscale homes that helped us gain a reputation for quality and elegance.

and got the financing together and closed the deal on Thursday. Later, Chris called me and said, "I want you to know I've made lots of deals in real estate. But the only one I've ever had close on the day agreed to in the contract was the one we just closed with you." We're still really good friends, and River Run was successful. It was the right time and the right place and the right product, so we sold lots to homebuilders in both River Run and Sunnyview while using some of the lots to build our own houses as well.

During the 1990s we developed a reputation for quality, using those home shows with our new name of Winton & Associates, Inc. Joy would decorate those models and we would meet with every customer. We usually got three to five contracts for pre-sales during the show and almost always sold our show home before the event was over. We were

heads above other builders with our designs and amenities and even if someone did not buy a home from us during that show, they would often come to us later to buy an existing home or have us design and build one for them. People used to tell me they have always wanted a Winton Home and never thought they could afford one. Well, now they can because we build in such diverse price ranges.

As we grew with numerous models in different parts of town, we began to have sales representatives staff the homes for us. They were told that their job was to give the solid prospects to me and I would make the sale. I had a lot of people learn how to close by watching me close their deals for them. Some are still very successful in El Paso real estate.

We were going along and things got better, but we were still feeling

the repercussions of the bankruptcy with our limited borrowing ability. A certain gentleman started hanging around the office, probably because he had to get out of the house, and one day he said, "You know, let me come and work for you and one day you will have the ability to borrow more money than you can use." That was Dan Rowe and he has been with us ever since. And what he predicted has come true. I think that he has had as much to do with the success of our company as anyone. He helps balance me and Herschel and he handles a lot of the things that I really don't like to do, things like records, details, personnel, filing deadlines and—in a lot of ways—the morale of the office staff. Sometimes he decides he is going to cook waffles for everyone. So he brings his collection of waffle irons to the office and lets Elsa Ortiz, our office manager, cook waffles for everyone.

A couple of years ago, Dan challenged the company to make a certain amount of sales. He promised that if we did, he would dress up as a woman for a day. The challenge amount seemed almost unattainable, considering what current sales were and the way the economy was floundering, so I do not think he expected to have to follow through with his

Dan Rowe, center, dressed as a woman, making good on a wager he lost when our sales goals exceeded his expectations. Accompanying Dan are Debbie and Herschel Stringfield.

end of the bargain. Well, we did make those sales and Dan did dress up. We had a party at the office and had our bankers come in to see it for themselves. To see our CFO acting like this at a time when things were not so positive for the economy really helped bring everyone's spirits up. The bankers loved it too, because it showed we had confidence in ourselves, we could have a good time in spite of the economy, and that we were hitting new sales goals.

I love Dan like a brother and we tease each other to the point of rudeness, just like brothers do who are so alike and yet so different. I think maybe it's because he has lived in a house full of women most of his life, like I did when I was growing up. He has three daughters; Angela Luttrell, his youngest, works with Dan. She is sharp, has her master's degree, and does a fantastic job for the company and a fantastic job of managing her dad. Both she and Dan also teach at the University of

Phoenix. I appreciate her loyalty and expect great things for her with the company.

> *There's a midget cowboy, and he keeps saying to the guy he works with, "My testicles hurt. I mean, it's really bad."*
>
> *His co-worker says, "Well, go to the doctor. It could be something really serious."*
>
> *Three days later the midget says, "Oh, man. I don't know if I can stand this. It really hurts."*
>
> *His co-worker says, "I told you go to the doctor."*
>
> *So, the midget finally does and the doctor picks the little guy up, and sets him up on the examining table.*
>
> *The doctor says, "Drop your pants and drawers down." He does. The doctor puts his hand there and says, "Turn your head and cough." So, he turned the other way and coughed. The doctor says, "Hmm, just a minute." He reaches over and picks up this pair of shears. The little guy's about to panic. The doctor goes clip, clip, clip, clip, clip, clip and says, "Now, pull your pants up, stand down and see how that feels."*
>
> *The midget gets down and says, "Wow, that feels good, and I didn't even feel anything. What'd you do?"*
>
> *The doctor says, "I cut two inches off the top of your cowboy boots."*

When we formed Flair Homes our intent was to build a high quality, semi-production home that could be less expensive than what our typical home would cost. We were building fantastic luxury homes, but we needed a way to attract buyers with a lower price point. Some of the sales reps would tell their prospects, "Hey, buy a Flair Home, it's a Winton." While it helped diversify our products, Flair eventually became a smaller custom Winton home. That helped us grow, and we sold homes that we might not have sold otherwise. Fortunately, we maintained

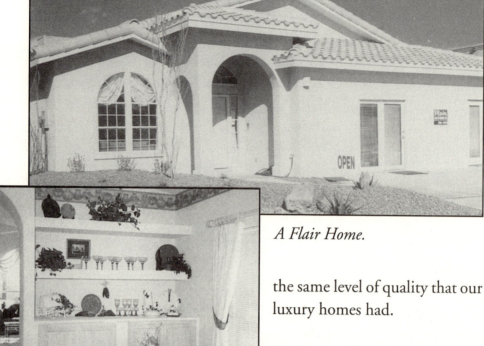

A Flair Home.

the same level of quality that our luxury homes had.

We became known in the development community as someone who could come and get a subdivision going. Laguna Meadows was a subdivision started by some lawyers as an investment. A group of doctors had made a loan to the attorneys as an investment. That loan was in a second lien position behind a bank, and when the bank posted the property for foreclosure, the doctors had to bid on the first lien to preserve their second lien, and they found themselves as the owner. They hired someone to manage the deal for them, but they were never able to get it going. We subsequently bought the development from the owners and completed the park and three additional phases. Laguna Meadows is one of the nicest developments in El Paso.

We also began to do more development. We had the opportunity to purchase some platted, unimproved subdivisions from Jim Scheer, a local attorney and real estate investor. We developed almost all of the subdivisions along Upper Valley Road between Gomez Road and

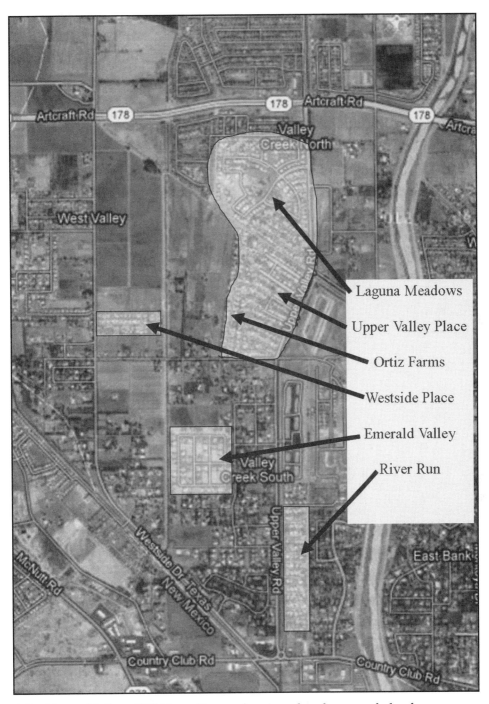

The Upper Valley of El Paso, Texas, showing the places we helped create.

Artcraft Road. We also developed some subdivisions on Westside Road and Gomez Road.

Sometime around the year 2000, I was discussing the Earl Nightingale program with someone and they asked if I still wrote my goals daily. I told them I didn't, but I made a decision then to begin using a new goal system. At the beginning of each year, I decide how much combined net profit of all the companies we want to earn. Napoleon Hill discusses ways to program your subconscious using repetition and autosuggestion, so now I structure a sentence, or a mantra, that has a cadence that matches my walking pace. Anytime I walk anywhere, I repeat that mantra in my head. When I first started, I said, " We will earn one million dollars in 2001." Each syllable is a footstep and as I walk I repeat the mantra. If I wake up in the night to go to the bathroom, I repeat that mantra as I walk. When I walk from my desk to the car, I repeat it. I repeat it every time I walk anywhere and I know exactly how many times I can repeat it for each particular regular walking trip that I will take during the day. By the end of the day, I will have said that mantra hundreds of times. By the end of the year, I will have repeated it hundreds of thousands of times. I do that every year with a new mantra and it works.

By the turn of the twenty-first century our business was going great. We had steady growth for ten consecutive years until the recession of 2008. During that time, our reputation grew as *the* quality builder in El Paso.

Have faith in yourself—and the quiet, firm, inner knowledge that you can and will accomplish your goals. Know that the answers you seek will come to you in their own time, if only you keep looking for them.

—Earl Nightingale

Thirty-seven

Accent on Success

I HAVE BEEN IN THE REAL ESTATE BUSINESS for fifty years, and I've learned that it is a roller coaster. So much depends on things beyond your control. Although we had nothing to do with the financial crash of 2008, it really could have hurt our business.

One person who helped us survive was Mark Dyer. His whole life has been connected in some way with homebuilding or building supplies. When I first met Mark around 1975, he was selling windows and handling other products for Arizona Wholesale Company, the Whirlpool Appliance distributor. Then he went to work for Jobe Concrete, a ready-mix concrete company, and when I hired him he was with Lone Star Title. But this guy has a way of pulling rabbits out of a hat. It is always surprising and it usually scares the hell out of me when he comes up with an idea.

It was his idea for us to build one hundred percent of our homes so they would qualify for an Energy Star rating. To earn the Energy Star, a home must meet the strict guidelines for energy efficiency set by the U.S. Environmental Protection Agency (EPA), making them twenty to thirty percent more efficient than standard homes. His thoughts were:

the government is doing free advertising for Energy Star. We should take advantage of that and align our branding with theirs. We were the first builder in El Paso to make the commitment to build one hundred percent of our homes Energy Star compliant. Now there are over 140 Energy Star builders in the region.

There was a development called Mason Farms located just on the edge—literally on the edge—of Texas in New Mexico. So Mark came to me and said, "You know they are developing these lots out there and I think that we ought to buy some."

I said, "Tell me about it." And he did.

I said, "Well go ahead and buy twenty lots and we'll try it."

"No, what I had in mind was to buy all of them, 124 of them."

"You're crazy, you're out of your mind."

Well, we bought all 124 of them and sold Energy Star houses on every lot. We never sold a lot to another homebuilder. We built all of them in a matter of about seventeen months. The original thinking was that the market would be for homes between twelve hundred and eighteen hundred square feet. Most of our sales there were for pre-sales and our range ended up being sixteen hundred and two thousand square feet. Prior to this, our average square footage home for the company was about twenty-eight hundred square feet. Building a smaller home again helped us diversify further and prepared us for Mark's next idea.

As we were winding up Mason Farms, the Base Closure and Realignment Commision process that the military goes through every few years established that Fort Bliss was going to go through a major expansion. BRAC is a government agency that aims to dispose of unnecessary United States Department of Defense (DoD) real estate. In the case of Fort Bliss, the closing of other bases around the world created consolidations that would cause Fort Bliss to grow tremendously.

Mark accurately predicted that we needed to get into a housing market I had not been in for many years: entry level. The military was expecting the bulk of the housing requirements for the twenty-four thousand soldiers coming into El Paso to be supplied by the local housing industry.

Mark's idea was to build a high-quality, Energy Star-rated home with a starting price close to a hundred thousand dollars. So he talked Herschel and I into starting Accent Homes. This idea is what allowed our company to stay in business at a high revenue level despite this great recession that began in 2008 and is still ongoing as this book is being written. The market for big homes actually dried up and went away, so we are grateful for Mark's idea.

We experienced a loss of sales when the economy began to crumble in late 2007 and throughout 2008. We flattened in 2009, and all the growth we've had since then has been in the Accent Homes division that Mark created. Research shows that Accent is the fourth largest volume builder in El Paso. The side effect of Accent's creation has also been the raising of standards for the other builders of entry-level homes for first-time buyers. So you could say that Mark has helped transform entry-level homebuilding in El Paso, while also helping our company grow.

I used to be indecisive.
Now I'm not so sure.

Over the years our company had developed a reputation for not being real friendly with the Realtor community. I guess the reputation was deserved in some ways, but so was our reluctance to embrace Realtors participation in our sales because of experiences we had with them in the past. I do not know how many times I got calls from Realtors on a Monday morning telling me that I needed to put their name on the contract I had written that weekend. They would explain that they had been working with that buyer for a certain period of time and that they had shown that buyer *x* number of homes and now that they had found one, the one I sold them over the weekend, they wanted to make sure I was going to pay them a commission. I never could understand why a

Realtor would think they were due a commission for the sale of a home they had never shown to the buyer. Now if they had brought the buyer to us, we would have gladly paid the commission. It did not take long before word got out that we refused to pay an unearned commission, and other Realtors did not want to do business with us.

I had empathy for the Realtors. I had been in their shoes before. I knew exactly how it felt to lose a prospect I had invested a lot of time in. I also knew how it hurt financially when I was depending upon that commission to help pay my bills. But I also knew it was my fault I was not getting a commission, because I knew there were things I probably could have done different to keep them as my buyer. I also never assumed that the seller of the home owed me anything if I didn't earn it. I never had a problem paying a commission to a Realtor who earned it by bringing their buyer to our office or model home, showing the prospect our product, helping make the sale, and helping manage the contract until closing.

I had lots of other scenarios where an unjustified commission was demanded or expected from Realtors, so I decided I would not go out of my way to cultivate Realtor business. This changed when I met Harold Newsom. He sold a couple of our houses when he was with Coldwell Banker and he had proved himself to be a Realtor who properly worked with his customers in helping them find the right home. He also was not a Realtor who expected something for nothing.

Mark Dyer had the idea that we get Harold to come on board and actually help cultivate Realtor business. I reluctantly agreed to it under one condition: I personally would not have to deal with Realtors. Harold pretty much kept to that agreement and it turned out to be a great strategy for our company. I was talking to Harold the other day and he told me he had counted up his sales with the company and it was nearly $115,000,000. Almost fifty percent of our total sales now are Realtor sales. We now enjoy a reasonable reputation with the Realtor community, and we are not paying unearned commissions.

Marty and I became interested in a piece of property that was directly across the street from what was originally the Horizon Country Club but is now called the Emerald Springs Golf Club. We bought the property and developed it into an upscale, gated subdivision. We sold lots to homebuilders and we built on some lots ourselves.

The club across the street was having major financial difficulties and subsequently went into foreclosure with the Bank of America. They had listed it with Roger Staubach's real estate company for some time and we took a look at it.

We'd had a little experience with the club business, mainly enough to know to stay away from it, but eventually—after Bank of America had been losing money for two years—the bank decided to close it up, turn off the power, turn off the water and let it grow up in weeds.

There were several families living around that old course and they got all excited about wanting to buy it because they didn't want it to close. They raised the funds, and they actually collected—not just pledged, but collected—a good amount of capital in a corporation called Friends of Emerald Springs (FOES). We didn't want it to close either, because our subdivision was right across the street.

It became a long drawn-out affair. FOES had us come and join with them and negotiate with Bank of America and finally after a lot of sweat and tears and late night phone calls we made the deal in my office with several FOES members present and the representative from Bank of America. Marty and I loaned them the money they needed and we now had the first lien on all of the 143 acres of land and the club house, driving range, swimming pool and golf course. The payments of ten percent interest a month have been coming in like clockwork.

Marty and I put together a lot of deals and you know the old saying, "If it ain't broke, don't fix it." So this relationship, this partnership, seemed to have some sort of a charmed life to it, and it worked so well that I really didn't want to change anything. Marty offers positive suggestions and support, but he has never questioned me. This relationship has caused us to establish a rule: If we don't control the checkbook, we will not be in the deal. We keep the checkbook, we keep the money, we do the accounting. Everybody we've partnered with has been agreeable to that and if they aren't agreeable, we won't do the deal with them.

Marty finally sold out of his property in Clovis and moved into the La Mesilla area outside of Las Cruces, New Mexico. He built his own home there about four years ago in a high end, one-acre lot subdivision we developed. He's also on our board in an advisory capacity. I asked him, "Now that you're down here, you have to sit in on our meetings because you make valuable contributions. What would it take to get you to work for me part time?"

And he said, "Oh, it's no problem. I'll do it on three conditions."

"Okay what are they?"

"One is that I don't have ownership of any kind, other than our development deals."

"Okay, what's next?"

"My office will be at my house."

"Okay. What's the other thing?"

"That you don't pay me anything."

Marty goes to all our board meetings and listens and contributes. He also comes when Scott and Todd and I do our twice-monthly Saturday morning tours. Marty says that his days as a homebuilder are over. But mine have just begun.

PEOPLE seem to be divided into those who understand that the wood must be put in the stove before they can expect warmth and those who feel they should get warmth whether or not they do anything about it, or who feel they should get maximum heat from too small a supply of wood.

—EARL NIGHTINGALE

PART VIII

Integrity

If we are true to ourselves, we cannot be false to anyone else. If our word to live by is integrity, we have what we need in a pinch, our sleep is untroubled, and we're respected wherever we go.

—Earl Nightingale

Thirty-eight

The First Key to Success: Our Product

You can't have a successful business unless you offer a great product. We provide the best quality, the best designs, the most energy efficient and the best value in homes in far west Texas, southern New Mexico and beyond. Period.

The keys to success in business have never really changed. You have to decide who you want to be in your particular industry and what you want to be known for and what level of service you want to provide. We decided that we wanted to be El Paso's leader in the high-quality affordable home market. We have succeeded in our goal. Today we are proud to say that we deliver superior homes at an affordable price.

One of the reasons we have been successful is that we stress quality in our product and expect our subcontractors to provide that quality. We use better materials and typically exceed building codes with our concrete, our framing techniques and our insulation.

We use energy efficient, low-E windows: low-emittance (low-E) coatings are microscopically thin, virtually invisible metal or metallic oxide layers deposited on a window or skylight glazing surface to reduce heat flow. We use high efficiency heating and cooling equipment and cellulose insulation that has a better R-value, a measure of thermal resistance used in the building and construction industry. Cellulose also maintains that R-value over a larger temperature spectrum and it seals the wall cavities better than fiberglass batts. Every one of our homes is third-party tested along with internal quality controls that help us minimize any defects in our products and processes.

Our Winton and Flair products provide a two-year warranty, bumper-to-bumper, that we give everybody, instead of the standard one year. We also send our maintenance people out to do a one-year "tune-up" approximately twelve months after their purchase. The tune-up checks the electrical, plumbing, and heating and cooling systems. We get up on the roof, we check the complete exterior envelope of the home. We make sure that the house is performing properly. And in any instance in which it is not, we'll take care of it, free. We like the homeowner to be there as well so we can show them the maintenance requirements of their home and how to perform that maintenance. Then we say, "It's your baby from now on."

We achieve Home Energy Rating System (HERS) scores that no other builder in the region achieves. To qualify as an Energy Star home, the third-party rater calculates a rating called HERS. The lower the number, the better. A zero-energy home, one that is not using any more energy than it is generating, would have a HERS score of zero. To qualify as an Energy Star home, you must have a score no higher than seventy-five. The scores on our homes have been between fifty-five and sixty-five for many years. We are way ahead of the competition.

We have an in-house design center that no one in the area has. Our custom buyers can come in and get their dream home designed before their very eyes. We have a drafting department that has been responsible for designing some of the nicest homes in the area. No one offers the

PHOTOGRAPH BY BILL FAULKNER

spectrum of pricing that we do or the diversity of locations. No one has the combined years of experience. Five or six of us were in a meeting at work the other day and we added up the combined experience of just those few individuals and we had over 250 years of combined experience in the real estate, development and homebuilding industries.

Probably the most important element we introduced into the El Paso market is green building. In fact, we have been one of the leaders in green building nationwide. We had the fifty-fifth Gold Certified Green Home in the country under the National Association of Home Builders rating system. Green refers to structure and building processes that are environmentally responsible and resource-efficient. New Mexico provides financial incentives in the form of income tax credits for builders to build green. Unfortunately, Texas does not have such an incentive program, so we have focused our green efforts in New Mexico.

We are proud to be part of the Build Green New Mexico program. To qualify for the program, a home has to have a certain number of points

PHOTOGRAPH BY BILL FAULKNER

in five categories: lot design preparation and development, resource efficiency, energy efficiency, water efficiency and pollutant source control, and operation maintenance and building owner education. To design our green homes, we looked for ways to get the biggest bang for our buck in achieving the points required. We meet with Javier Ruiz, our third party rater, to discuss advancements in energy saving features such as energy-saving dishwashers, windows and tankless hot water heaters.

One of the key factors in energy efficient building is insulation. Insulation minimizes infiltration and helps keep houses cooler in the summer and warmer in the winter. We only use the highest quality cellulose insulation that is carefully applied for maximum efficiency. When we realized that our insulation subcontractors were not giving us the service we needed, we started a company called Comfort Control, and we now do our own insulating. Our company does great work.

Our homes are all third-party tested, and their energy efficiency is twice as good as it has to be to be under the current building codes. We give people a written guarantee of the approximate costs they can expect to heat and cool their home. If it costs more than the guarantee, we pay them the difference for the first two years.

We also built the first home in the area to receive a zero energy rating. It has solar cells on the roof that turn sunlight into electricity. In New Mexico, they use a dual metering system where the electric company pays you for the electricity generated from your solar panels. The home also has a solar water heating system as well. The hot water is used during the winter for heating the home, in addition to heating water year round for domestic consumption. To put it in simple terms, this means that the homeowners will have a net energy cost of zero dollars for electricity and gas over the course of a year.

The EPA has nationally recognized our efforts five years in a row, between 2006–2010. We had the honor of receiving the Energy Star Partner of the Year award for two consecutive years. We also received a national

Energy Star award for promotion of the brand and we received two Sustained Excellence awards. Herschel traveled to Washington D.C. numerous times to receive these awards. He described the experience as not too unlike the Academy Awards ceremony. According to Herschel, the presenter of the award said that he was sitting with the committee to decide who was going to be the Energy Star Partner of the Year in the builder category for the entire United States. After the committee reviewed our application, they turned to one another and said, "Who are these people? Did they come from outer space? What's the deal?"

> *A lady comes up to the drug store. She goes to the back to the pharmacist. "Do you sell Viagra in here?"*
> *He said, "Yes, ma'am. We do."*
> *She said, "Does it really work?"*
> *"Yes, ma'am, it does."*
> *"How do you know?"*
> *"Okay, I take it. I have tried it."*
> *"Well, can you get it over the counter?"*
> *He said, "If I take two I can."*

We have been innovators in other ways as well. There are so many things that we brought to the El Paso market that other builders have adopted. One is the upper storage shelving you now see in many garages. We were the first to start doing that in the '80s. We also introduced the wall of built-in sheetrock shelves you see in a lot of builders' homes. We call it the Winton Wall. Joy and I used to go to other markets a couple of times a year to get new ideas. We would bring ideas here from other parts of the country, usually Las Vegas, Nevada, or Arizona.

Recently we teamed up with Dusty Henson at the El Paso Saddleblanket Company to create a new concept: homes that offer a southwestern interior design. We call it El Paso Saddleblanket Branded Homes. It is a novel concept based upon Dusty's perspective that, "The Southwest is the signpost where the Cowboy, Indian and Mexican come together

PHOTOGRAPH BY BILL FAULKNER

in culture. It represents a lifestyle as romantic as a Mexican fiesta and as rough and ready as rodeos and rattlesnakes. It is a daydream that still lives here..." We developed it as something that would appeal to people wanting to retire to the Southwest. The recession hit, the stock market shrank and evaporated most people's retirement funds about the time we developed the concept. When retiree relocation to El Paso resumes on a greater level, we expect sales of these homes to increase.

Delivering such high quality products can be stressful at times. It requires carrying a lot of overhead. We have managed over the years to consistently meet our overhead and put the earnings back into the company. That is what has allowed us to grow. The size of our company, with approximately sixty-five employees, allows us to provide the level of service we promise. It is also what allows us to offer seller financing in selective instances to people who would not otherwise be able to purchase a new home.

One of the ways we are able to offer decent prices to our customers is that we keep our costs low. For instance, the electric company came out with a program for putting solar cells to generate electricity on commercial buildings. So, we revamped our office building with these photovoltaic cells and we cut our electric bill dramatically. It may seem like a little thing but it is important to us to run the most efficient operation possible. We also are constantly working with our subcontractors and suppliers to insure we are getting the best value for our dollar. We take advantage of every prompt payment discount offered and we get some of the best interest rates on our interim loans from our lenders.

> *We're like the attorney who said, "I have never lost a case."*
> *I said, "Are you telling me that in twenty-nine years you have never lost a case?"*
> *And he said, "No, I never have. Now, my client has often been convicted, but I always got paid."*

What a lot of people do not realize is that there is a lot of risk in the homebuilding business. We are sometimes required to make commitments on lots that can't be built on for a year or more. So many things can change in that time that would affect the housing market. Once the lots are ready to be built on, it takes anywhere from three to five months to complete the home—again, a long time before you are in a position to close on that home. Many things can happen on pre-sale homes between the time of contract and closing: there is the risk that the buyer won't qualify by the time the house is finished or that something will happen that keeps them from being able to close. If it is a spec house, the risk is even greater. What if we picked the wrong lots? What if we misjudged the market and built a house that was too expensive or too small? What if our plan has flaws and doesn't sell? All of those issues are a risk.

One of the keys to success in homebuilding is successful financing. We were fortunate in having enough bank relationships to do this. Dan Rowe, our chief financial officer, has a way of dealing with banks and bankers. There was a time when things were really going great in '06 and many banks were courting us for our business. I was even able to get a zero-zero financing deal: prime plus zero and no origination fee. Having relationships with many banks competing for our business insured us getting the best rates.

So we had all these banks lined up that way. Then this current recession came along and banks cut way back on their lending. Fortunately for us we have maintained relationships with multiple banks, so if one decides to curtail their interim construction lending, we have others we can use. I have seen builders go broke because they only worked with one bank. If the bank changed their rules, or would not renew interim loans, then the builder was stuck. But we are in good shape because at least we can still get loans. There are a lot of builders who are out of business because they cannot borrow money. But it is our history of always paying on time that has allowed us to continue to get financing.

So how do I sleep at night, knowing all of those things? I sleep like a baby…I wake up crying every three hours. Seriously, I know I have competent people, I know I have good processes for helping insure the right decisions, and I have an intuition developed, through fifty years of experience with numerous economic cycles and one bankruptcy, in how to manage and minimize risk.

We must walk with integrity every day of our lives, if we are to reap the abundant harvest all the years of our lives.

—Earl Nightingale

Thirty-nine

The Second Key to Success: Our People

Of course, the biggest reason for our success, and the success of any company, is people. When I am looking for someone to join our company, I look for a people person, someone who is able to concentrate on giving people good quality service and taking care of the customer. That's what we have to do in our homebuilding business. We have a lot of good people working at the company in all different positions. I cannot mention them all, but I'm proud of the work they do.

I have already mentioned some of the key players in our company who have been doing a great job for years. First and foremost is my terrific partner, Herschel Stringfield. Dan Rowe and Mark Dyer have also been essential to the success of our company because of their tremendous people skills.

When we were at Western Skies patio homes in the ealry '80s, we had a high school student join us part time under a school to work program. Her name was Letty Mata, and she would ride the city bus from the Lower Valley and back every day. She has been with us ever since and is our chief designer. She has developed a skill of being able to work with our high-end buyers from the start to the finish of their home. She also runs the drafting department, which makes her job one of the most important in the company. First, she has to be able to determine from the customers the things they want in their home and she has to translate that into plans that can be built by our people out in the field. Secondly, she has to be able to match the buyer's price limitations and make sure we can sell the house for what it needs to be sold for. This is based upon the components of the house in developing the construction budget. Third, she has to distribute those plans, first to the buyers and get the final approval, and then to the roof truss designer, the foundation designer, any architectural approval committees, the City for permits, the various internal departments we have in the company, and to the superintendent and foremen who will oversee the job and the subcontractors and suppliers who will work on the home. That is a lot of responsibility because when something is not right it causes a lot of problems. Letty has two great guys working for her as well, Abraham De Leon and Miguel "Tito" Flores. Both are in our scholarship program and Abraham is studying architecture.

Another fantastic person who has been with us a long time is Ivonne Moreno. She started seventeen years ago as a receptionist and runs our accounts payable department. That is a critical department for us because part of our success is based upon paying people promptly. Our subs know that we pay on time and they appreciate that, so we get better service. Our suppliers know we pay on time so we get better pricing as well as prompt-payment discounts. Ivonne makes that happen. She handles thousands of invoices a month and is always on top of things.

We have had others who started as a receptionist and have worked their way into other departments. Brianna Concha, who helps Angela Luttrell, did that about five years ago. Elsa Ortiz also started as a receptionist ten years ago. Her brother was looking for a house when we had the chance to meet Elsa and her husband, Joe. During the process of helping her brother, I suggested that maybe she and Joe were ready for a new home, and they agreed. So we built them a beautiful home on the golf course. I learned that Elsa is very sharp, so I suggested that maybe she and her family were at a stage where she might be ready to go back to work. She said she was, so she hired on as a receptionist, then moved to accounts payable, then moved to purchasing, then quality and now she acts as office manager and closing coordinator. Her fantastic people skills help keep everyone sane during what could be a tense time: closing on a new home. Elsa also takes great care of me by readying my office with the right temperature, fresh water and nice music for my daily arrival. She helps me with the computer too, when it won't do what it's supposed to!

Raul Chavez is another one who has been with us for a long time. He joined us as a superintendent and is now in charge of all of our construction. He has trained a great team of superintendents and foremen so that we can build a top quality home. He has also instilled in his people the right attitude in dealing with our customers so that Raul's team helps make the homebuilding experience as enjoyable as possible. I have also found that Raul is a person I can depend upon to get things done. I have overloaded him at times, but he comes through like a champ. One of his lieutenants is his son Raul, Jr. He has been working for us since he was in high school and is now in charge of our insulation company. He also has oversight of construction on his father's behalf. The Chavez family is a vital component to our success.

Another key person is Edmundo "Mundo" Dena, who we hired from a large homebuilding company. He's thirty-five years old now and he's got about twenty years experience in the homebuilding business. His father was, and still is, a sheetrock contractor. Edmundo was out there nailing sheetrock when he was about fourteen years old. He's a good young man, and he runs Accent Homes. Mundo is becoming a top-notch business manager with the potential for success similar to Herschel's. He brought an experience and perspective that we did not have previously, and that is how to build production homes. We grew from a custom home business, he grew from a production home business. I think the two backgrounds have helped Accent provide a level of quality you normally do not see in production homes because of our custom home roots. Without Mundo, Accent Homes would not be the fourth largest builder in the El Paso area. That is a lot considering it happened in less than five years and the builders who are bigger than Accent have all been in business longer than twenty-five years.

Mundo has his own management meetings on Tuesday mornings which I sometimes attend. I listen in a little bit and pitch a comment or two in the air, but there is really no connection between Accent and the rest of the company. We don't even use the same accounting system. We bought an accounting and workflow management system called Builder MT for Accent Homes. This system allows a builder to have a paperless operation when fully utilized. We hired Vivian Alvarado from another company where they had Builder MT and she runs it and keeps up with everything.

> *There's a story about the real estate salesman whose friend asked him, "How's business?" And he said, "Well let me see, I sold a house on Monday. I didn't do anything on Tuesday. On Wednesday the deal on the house I sold on Monday fell through. So I guess Tuesday was my best day."*

About six years ago, my son Todd joined the company, initially to help implement the Builder MT computer program for Accent Homes. But what he had always wanted to do was quality inspections for our homes. Todd is good at giving unique and critical attention to detail, and he inspects every one of our homes. In some product lines he performs three to four inspections on each home. Since he has taken over this job, our quality has gotten better and our subcontractors have learned to perform to a higher standard because there is a Winton inspecting their work. His eye on the Accent product and a willingness from the Accent people to learn from him has caused the Accent quality to be the best in the production home market in El Paso. I am proud of the work Todd does, because quality is what our business has been built on, and he is the one who helps insure that quality.

My second oldest son, Scott, joined the company about seven years ago. He has served as sales manager a couple of times, handles our city relations, deals with special customers, writes letters that need special attention, helps with sales when necessary, and manages the land-development part of the business. He has a unique and diverse background in real estate, land development and municipal government and uses those experiences in whatever capacity is needed. His prior tenure as mayor of Pflugerville, Texas, has prepared him for his varied duties in our company. His current projects include developing Rio Valley, a subdivision that uses Smart Growth principles, and the Piazza Escondida, a small mixed-use condo development we are building next door to our office. Smart Growth is an urban planning and transportation theory that concentrates growth in compact walkable urban centers to avoid sprawl.

> *A young man was called into the company president's office. The president told him, "You have done an outstanding job, you are punctual and productive and we are promoting you to vice president. The young man reached across the president's desk to shake his hand and said, "Thanks, dad."*

My grandson Mark joined the company selling homes about five years ago while also pursuing a degree in architecture. Even though he was successful at sales, once he graduated he expressed a desire to learn other parts of the business. He is now in our purchasing department still wishing to learn more parts of the company. I expect him to grow into a person capable of running the entire business one day.

We have lots of other great people that I could devote chapters to who have not been mentioned yet. To acknowledge our appreciation to them they are listed on page 252 along with the years they have been with us.

Above—Me with my grandson Mark Winton.
Right—Me and my son Todd who is by far the best quality inspector I have ever seen.

We take care of the people who work for us. We had an instance where the bank that we run our operating checking accounts through began to charge a fee for cashing checks. I told them "I'll tell you what, we're not gonna do any business with you. We're going to move all of our accounts out of there unless you change. Our employees and our contractors need to get their cash without your deducting a fee."

They said, "Well, everybody charges this fee."

I said, "No, everybody doesn't."

"Bank of America does and Wells Fargo does."

"We don't do business with either one of them for our local operating accounts. So what are you gonna do?"

So this guy sits there for a minute in a meeting which happened to be at our office, and he had brought three other officers with him.

Twenty-six years:	Leticia Mata
Twenty years:	Raul Chavez Sr., Dan Rowe, Jesus "Chuy" Robles
Seventeen years:	Ivonne Morneo
Thirteen years:	William "Billy" Najera
Twelve years:	Raquel Martinez Wood, Raul Chavez Jr.
Eleven years:	Elsa Ortiz
Ten years:	Mark Dyer, David Blackmon
Nine years:	Oscar Castillo, Jessica Sanchez, Angela Luttrell
Eight years:	Cesar Chavez, Miguel "Tito" Flores, Antonio "Tony" Martinez, Cesar Aguirre, Jose Carmona, Scott Winton, Clint Newsom, Edd Merrell
Seven years:	Francisco "Javier" Bocanegra, Luis "Enrique" Tovar, Abraham De Leon
Six years:	Jorge Gamboa, Leopoldo "Polo" Linares, Gaspar Marquez, Samuel Munoz, Raul Ramirez, Todd Winton, Edmundo "Mundo" Dena, Mark Winton
Five years:	Adriana Hernandez, Brianna Concha, Vivian Alvarado, Projedis Ortiz, Adolpho Hernandez, Jose Luis Herrera
Four years:	Michael Carrasco, Steven Muniz, Henry Bone
Three years:	Marcos Martinez, Ines Rubalcaba, Santiago Rangel, Samuel Dominguez, Ivan Munoz, Jose Marquez, Cesar De La Riva
Two years:	Emily Bondhus, Dennis Wheeler, Linda Thomas, Pedro Puente, Leticia Navarro, Norma Renz
One year:	Krystal Ortiz, Mauricio Holguin, Maria "Sandra" Blancas, Veronica Martinez, Humberto Lopez, Danny De La Riva, Daniel Delgado, Alex Solot, Carol Esco, Jesus Beltran, Oscar Macias
Eight Months:	Rosemary Rhodes
Seven Months:	Luis Armando Cadena
Six Months:	Daniel Josue Tovar, Erica Silva

A HARD WORKING GROUP OF PEOPLE *outside our office on Escondido Drive. That's me, seated upfront. Behind me, from left to right:* **Row 1**—*Debbie Stringfield, Herschel Stringfield, Dan Rowe, Todd Winton, Scott Winton, Raul Chavez Sr.* **Row 2**—*Dennis Wheeler, Linda Thomas, Anna Ruiloba, Carla Bentancourt, Desiree Diaz, Veronica Martinez, Brianna Concha, Angela Luttrell, Ivonne Moreno.* **Row 3**—*Elsa Ortiz, Krystal Ortiz, Maria Sandra Blancus, Emily Ann Bondhus, Vivian Alvarado, Adriana Hernandez, Letty Mata, Jessica Sanchez.* **Row 4**—*Santiago Rangel, Leopoldo Linares, Raul Chavez Jr., Chuy Robles, William Najera, Abraham De Leon.* **Row 5**—*Raul Ramirez, Luis Armando Cadena, Tony Martinez, Oscar Castillo, Mike Carrasco, Jorge Gamboa.* **Row 6**—*Samuel Dominquez, Ines Rubalcava, Pedro Puente.* **Row 7**—*Enrique Tovar, Mark Dyer, Javier Bocanegra, Mike Hiett, Samuel Munoz.* **Row 8**—*Danny De La Riva, Cesar De La Riva, Cesar Aguirre, Miguel Flores, Jose Carmona.*

They all kind of looked at each other. He said, "Well, I guess we won't charge any longer for people who cash your checks."

Two days later our CFO went to cash a check and they tried to charge him ten dollars. But that was the last time.

We believe in paying bonuses to our employees. I believe that in addition to salaries, bonuses are important so that people know they are the ones who made our success possible. It's justifiable that they should share in the benefits. One year we paid over $700,000 to employees in bonuses. Some of the people got a bonus check of almost half of their salary for the year.

I have a big jar at my office called "The Chairman's Ballgame." It is filled with plastic eggs. Employees, who have been recognized for good service by customers in a letter, are brought into a meeting with a crowd of his or her peers watching. We read the letter, give the deserving employee an "attaboy," and let them reach in and pull out an egg. When opened the egg reveals a piece of paper with an amount written anywhere from one hundred to one thousand dollars. Fellow workers can also recommend others to "pull an egg" when they see someone doing great things.

I believe that if anyone shows initiative and spark, he or she deserves to be given a chance to succeed. I also believe strongly in a college education. For that reason, we have given many employees college scholarships. Last year two employees graduated from college and we have four more in school now. They have to get the course approved for reimbursement by their manager, and if they make a B or better we reimburse them the tuition.

We throw a family party every year for all of the employees and their immediate families, which is always a lot of fun. We have held it at Western Playland, Wet N' Wild, Water World and Incredible Pizza. We've also held the party at bowling alleys that have indoor entertainment areas. We've even held the party in Marty's huge backyard. In 2011 we went to Adventure Zone. I think everyone enjoyed that the best. They closed

Having fun at a Family Day party at Marty Shaeffer's house.

the place for us and we got unlimited food, games and rides. They let us bring our own beer too. We went there again for our 2012 party and rented the entire facility for the Friday night party.

Herschel Stringfield remains the soul of the company. So let me tell you what I have learned in twenty-eight years of dealing with Herschel. He is steady, he's quiet and he brings a calmness to the operation. He works hard, he is detail oriented. He starts every morning at about seven and works until about six every evening. He puts in ten and eleven hour days daily and in the process he has managed our business and made himself a nice net worth. He has the financial ability to do anything he wants to, any time. He can afford it. And he still lives fairly conservatively. He and Debbie live in a very nice home that they built for themselves about eight years ago. While partnering with Herschel I have also been fortunate to watch Herschel and Debbie's two children, Nathan and Tiffany, grow into outstanding adults.

Mark Dyer and myself before one of the cookouts we sponsor for our sales people when they hit certain sales goals. Mark is one of the best steak cookers I know.

Gradually, Herschel began making all the key decisions. For example, I can be sitting in my office reading *Time* magazine and Herschel will be in his office looking at contracts. The salesmen all bring their contracts to him and he makes the call: do we or don't we accept this deal. He looks at the closing statements and signs off on them and deeds all the properties to buyers. He's a first class guy, he's young enough, fifty-five, that if we ever decided to go public, he is in a position to handle it. I fully trust him with the entire operation of the company.

The most important thing I have learned is the necessity of reasonableness. The person who has the least to regret, who does most for his community, whose judgment carries the most weight and is the most trusted, is the person who is steadfastly and on principle reasonable.

—EARL NIGHTINGALE

Forty

The Most Important Key to Success: Our Customers

Through sixty some years in business, nothing has ever been more important to me than my customers. When I was selling shoes, I always listened to my customers to understand exactly what they wanted. When I was selling meat, I took the time to get to know butchers, short order cooks and managers. When I was selling real estate, I did the same with my customers. Since I've been in the homebuilding business, I have always made customer service my highest priority. All of us at Winton Homes are "people people." We love serving people. My motto has always been:

RTPSF / RWF
Remember To Put Service First / Rewards Will Follow

Nothing has been more important to the success of our business than our customers. We pride ourselves in delivering excellent service to everyone from the young family buying their first house to the successful executive looking for his dream home. We always put the needs of our customers first and work with them to find the right home at the right price.

I recently had an opportunity to deal with a customer who came into the office and I said, "Tell me about yourself. How long have you and your family lived in El Paso? What do you do for a living? How many children do you have? How many of them have gone to school here?" I am genuinely and truly interested. Just like in the book by Dale Carnegie that Mr. Norman, my geometry teacher in high school, suggested that the class read. The best part is, I remember the people I meet, and the things they have told me about themselves. And it is always a joy to see them and get caught up on their lives.

> *I've had people ask, "Did you ever play golf?"*
> *And I said, "If you ever saw what I did and then asked if I was playing golf, I'd ask you if you were crazy."*

There was a terrible freeze in February 2011. El Paso had not seen it that cold in over fifty years. People's pipes were freezing all over the region. The utility companies were having brownouts and there were people without water, heat and lights everywhere. Our homes fared quite well through this. But some customers had irrigation backflow preventers freeze, some had tankless water heaters ice up, and some had condensation lines from their high efficiency furnaces freeze up. Compared to other builders, our homeowners had very few problems.

Afterwards the city made some code changes. One recommendation was for builders to use PEX piping since it withstands freeze breaking. We had already been using that for years. We made some of our own changes including placing our tankless water heaters on interior walls. We also now run the condensation lines to an indoor drain pipe, rather than outside.

Through this regional deep freeze, our company was the only one to shine. We stopped all construction so we could concentrate on helping our customers. We had a command center at our office with three people manning the phones. We had our warranty people and our superintendent and foreman in all parts of town. When calls would come in, we would dispatch the person closest to the problem to respond.

Other builders in town responded a little differently. One told his homebuyers that it was an act of God and he could not, or would not, help. Some didn't answer their phones and even took their phone number off of their webpage. They continued with their ongoing building projects, too.

Sometimes people ask us to do a little too much. During this freeze Mark Dyer took a call from a person who said, "You need to get over here and help me get my water line unfrozen." Mark asked, "What is your address?" When he gave it, Mark said, "I don't remember us building a house on that street." And the caller said, "You didn't build my house, so and so did, but they won't come out." "Well why are you calling us?" Mark asked. The caller said, "Because you built my sister's house and you had her water working in ten minutes."

We had another person call and say, "Please come fix my furnace." We asked the address and had to tell her we didn't build her home. "Why are you calling us?" "Because my builder won't answer the phone and your guy is right down the street." The sad part about this story is that we were also right down the street when she was buying her home from a builder that did not have a focus on customer service.

Every customer gets a gift basket at the home closing. In that gift basket we put all sorts of goodies, ranging from stuff they can use on move-in day to neat decorating items. We also include an envelope containing the specific Energy Star results of their HERS rating that was carried out by the independent third party.

Last week I got two letters from people that said, "We've lived in different places. We have dealt with different homebuilders and owned many new homes. We have never been treated as well as the way your people treated us." And they specifically name a particular individual, adding that, "This person went above and beyond the call of duty."

That is what we all strive to do.

*O*UR POPULATION *is getting a lot smarter. Educational advances during the past thirty years have been remarkable. During the next thirty, they'll probably be amazing! The customer is getting smarter every day. And if we're going to continue to meet his demands and sell him our products, we'd better get smarter every day, too.*

—EARL NIGHTINGALE

Forty-one

Non-Stop Learning

THROUGHOUT MY LIFE, I have always enjoyed learning new things. In recent years, as business has stabilized, I have realized traveling is a wonderful way to learn.

One of our most memorable trips was in 2001. Joy and I and the Shaeffers made a trip around the world. We had to travel in one direction all the time. We were gone two months, traveled over seventy thousand miles, went to six continents, thirteen separate countries, and stayed as long as we wanted to in any particular place. American Airlines offered a program called *oneworld*, which partnershiped with airlines all over the world, and we were able to get first-class air transport for what was quite a reasonable sum. Under the program you were allowed to make up your own schedule, but you always had to keep traveling in the same direction until you had gone around the world.

Joy worked on putting this trip together for two months. She's excellent at arranging everything. At every stop, when we would get off the plane, there'd be somebody standing on the concourse holding up a sign with our name on it. There was a limo outside to take us to

Vacation time with friends. Couples, left to right: Joy and me, Ellen Claire and Marty Shaeffer, Tommie and Dan O'Leary, Patricia and Ramiro Saenz.

the local InterContinental Hotel and up to the concierge level. Marty and I would drink 'em out of Scotch, I think, but the brand that they generally served was Teacher's. One afternoon we had been out touring and we came through the lobby. I said, "Let's stop in here and have a drink." He said, "Well, they got 'em upstairs." And I said, "I know, but let's go in here."

So we go in the bar. It's a beautiful, plush place. And each of us had a Scotch and the bill was thirty dollars.

So we realized what a bargain we had been getting at the concierge level.

> *During World War II two Jewish guys decide they are going to assassinate Hitler. They manage to get a copy of his schedule so they know where he is supposed to be at eleven*

o'clock and they are waiting for him. Eleven o'clock comes and he hasn't shown up. Eleven-thirty comes and he hasn't shown up. At about twelve o'clock he still hasn't shown up. One of them looks at the other and says, "Gee, I hope nothing happened to him!"

We stopped in Vienna, Austria. In fact, we went to the main show that evening, the presentation of music in the music hall. Ellen Claire made a few of these reservations. She's into music big time, played the violin and the piano and sang in the church choir. She had asked for the "best seats available." So we had the best seats. We were in a box seat looking right down at the orchestra and the stage.

The next day we got a driver to tour the surrounding countryside and when we got back to the hotel, around three in the afternoon, we decided we'd lay down and take a little nap before we started our evening by going up to the concierge lounge.

I had just lain down on the bed and the phone rang. It was Marty. He said, "You got your TV on?"

I said, "No."

"Turn it on."

"Why?"

He said, "Somebody just bombed the World Trade Center in New York City."

I said, "Marty, this is a little early in the day to start that kind of crap. Take a nap. Enjoy yourself. I'll see you later."

"No, I'm serious. Turn on your TV." I turned the TV on just in time to see the second airplane hit the second Tower.

That evening we went to the lounge where they had a fourteen piece orchestra set up, and they weren't even playing. The musicians were just sitting in their chairs. The place was empty, everyone had gone home to watch TV. There was just a handful of people at the bar all huddled around the TV.

We occupied a booth and sat there and they finally came and waited

I was surrounded by birds in this plaza in Venice.

on us and we ordered a drink. Eventually one lone violinist got up from the chair, came and stood right in front of us and began playing American songs.

Wherever we went people just came up and took us by the hand and said, "I am so sorry."

I have heard people say how they don't like Americans in Europe. That's not true. We went all over the world and everywhere we went people were nice. That was quite a trip. We had plane reservations to fly from Vienna back to London and change planes to go to Prague in the Czech Republic. We forfeited our airline tickets for that segment and took the train because of all the airport closings.

Prague is the most beautiful, unbelievable architectural marvel and it was somehow spared in World War II. None of that city was bombed. It is gorgeous, and we went all over. We hired a driver and a guide, and they sent a good-sized van that would hold twelve or fourteen people for just the four of us. They were showing us the city and they took us to a square. We were marveling at all these beautiful buildings and it was raining slightly. All of a sudden a bell started tolling and everybody—there were probably 150 people on that square—and everybody stopped what they were doing and bowed their heads. The bell continued to ring for what was two minutes.

We asked the guide, "What's going on?" He said this was an announced event, two minutes of silence worldwide, to show homage to the people who were killed in the World Trade Center bombing. All over the world, that's what was going on.

It's amazing how close everyone in the world has become. And it's been our joy to have met so many wonderful people all over the world.

> *There's three couples on a cruise ship. They're assigned to have all their meals together. Two of them are young couples on their honeymoon and the other one is a couple who's been married for over thirty years. The very first morning at breakfast this one groom comes to his little bride and says, "Would you like some honey, Honey?"*
>
> *The other one, not to be outdone, turns to his bride and says, "Would you like some sugar, Sugar?"*
>
> *The third man turns to his wife and says, "Would you like some bacon, Pig?"*

One of our experiences on this trip was a photo safari at the Mala Mala Game Preserve in South Africa. It was amazing. In a three-day safari I took 625 photos of animals, and we celebrated my sixty-eighth birthday while there. We had a great party. The entire group participated, everybody who was on that safari trip. They started off with about twenty servers walking into the room with food—huge platters on top of their heads, and many of 'em had flambé dishes. It was a most memorable sixty-eighth birthday. I don't think I could have a better birthday than that one.

Some years ago, Marty and Ellen Claire Shaeffer, Mike Williams and his wife Pat, and Joy and I all took a tour of England and Scotland. We went to the famous St. Andrews golf course, and Marty and I, having been in that business, were curious about the course. We walked into the pro shop. It had a very large circular countertop with a golf pro behind it. And we said, "It's a windy, blustery day and not many people playing. Could we walk out on the course for a moment?"

The golf pro said, "Oh, certainly, mon. You want to walk on the old course or the new course?"

And I said, "A new course? I didn't realize you had a new course."

"Oh yes, mon. We do have."

"Well, when was it built?"

"Oh, two hundred years ago."

"Two hundred years ago? How 'bout the old course?"

"Oh, mon, that was built six hundred years ago," and then he said, "You know the problem with you blokes from the colonies is that you don't have any history."

Traveling has also taught us about our family heritage. My sister Louise, when she was in her seventies, decided to conduct some genealogical studies and found that the first Winton to come to the United States was from Scotland. There were two brothers and they were not pleased with the way things were going in Scotland, so they left. One of them settled on the East Coast and one on the West Coast. We supposedly are descendants of the brother from the East Coast.

We met some friends many years later from Edinburgh. And they said, "Have you ever been to Scotland? You ought to go eighteen to twenty miles east of Edinburgh and see what you find."

"What will I find?" I asked.

"You'll find the little town of Winton."

So, when we went to Edinburgh on vacation, we were driving along and saw a huge billboard that read, "Entering New Winton, drive carefully." We stopped at the Winton Arms and asked the bartender and others, "Why is it called New Winton?"

"Oh, because Old Winton burned, the entire town burned."

"Oh, where is it?"

"It's about three miles down the road. It was rebuilt here. Have you seen the Winton Castle?"

We drove out to it and sure enough, saw this huge building. We met a fellow at the castle who was getting his Ph.D. in Scottish History. We sat out on a bench under a tree, and he told us the history of the castle. He said it was built in the year 1022. One of its most famous inhabitants was the Earl of Winton who originally started out as a blacksmith and made the strongest swords in the land. Whenever his men were planning a foray, they'd say, "We have to put Winton in the front line because he is equal to any four men."

Besides traveling, reading is my favorite hobby. One of my favorite places to read is at the fishing camp that my friend Marty Shaeffer has had in Colorado for almost forty years. A trout stream runs through the property. This place is located so high up in the mountains it gets six to ten feet of snow in the winter time. Marty opens the camp every year in May and usually closes it in October. So he gets five or six useable months out of it, and it is beautiful.

Marty is a fisherman's fisherman. Once at dinner time, he asked everyone how many trout could each eat and what size of fish they preferred. Everyone put in their orders. Marty reached up and took a fancy fishing rod from a rack, strapped on his little creel and says, "I'll be back shortly." He went down to the stream and I'm not kidding you, he came back in forty-five minutes with the correct number of fish of the correct size.

I am no fisherman. As I said, I like to read books. One day, everybody was gone off riding in Jeeps or fishing or hiking. There were little chipmunks everywhere. They were looking for whatever food you might happen to drop. I took a package of trail mix with peanuts, and I knew

Marty and Ellen Claire Shaeffer at the fishing camp in the 1980s. Kristel is in front seat with them and Monica is in the back with Marty's boy Dan and Mitch and Gary Simms. Marty got that Jeep when he was in high school.

where the chipmunks were underneath the mobile home. I laid little dabs of food to create a trail from the hole in the skirting. Pretty soon, sure enough, they'd come out and grab some food, look up at me, and go back under the skirting again. Then they'd come back out and come a little closer and a little closer. This took about two hours.

And finally I set up a trail that led to me. I stood a piece of firewood near my knee and put some food on top of it, and then I put some on my knee and then I would hold some food in my hand. Honestly, I had two of these little chipmunks, one on each knee, just arguing like hell about who was allowed to be there and they were giving each other hell. And I'm sitting there just dying laughing. They ate all the food I had put out. One of them ran up on my knee and looked at me and had an

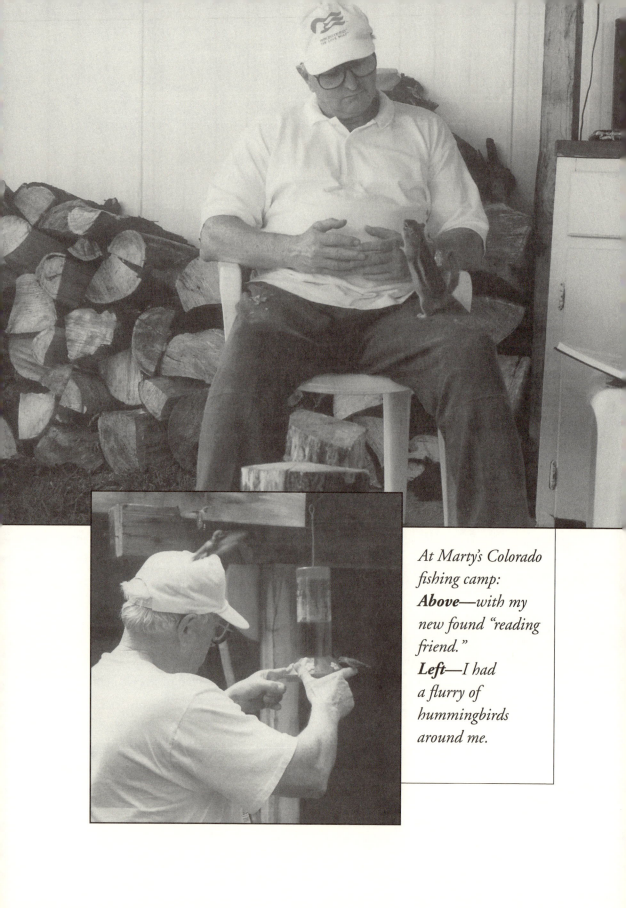

At Marty's Colorado fishing camp: **Above**—with my new found "reading friend." **Left**—I had a flurry of hummingbirds around me.

expression that said, "What's going on?" I had my hand closed a bit and he came over with his little hand and he started unfolding my fingers. And sure enough, I had a peanut in there. When he saw the peanut, he grabbed it and looked up at me as if to say, "Ah ha, I got it!"

The next morning, Joy said, "I guess you're going to spend the day fiddling with those chipmunks." And I said, "No, they've got a little bitty brain about the size of a BB and I don't want to take two hours to retrain the little buggers." So I got me a nice comfortable place and a book and sat down, and I'm reading this book and all of a sudden I feel something. I slowly moved the book over to see what it was. Sitting on my knee is one of those little chipmunks looking up at me with an expression of: "Well?"

I feel like St. Francis of Assisi when I go there. I have even had hummingbirds land on my finger.

A priest went fishing, and he caught the damnedest fish about two feet long, a beautiful fish. He started back to the monastery and met one of the parishioners who says, "Oh, my goodness, Father. That is the most beautiful son of a bitch I ever saw."

And the priest said, "Sir, I'm a man of the cloth. You shouldn't talk like that around me."

"You don't understand? That's the name of this fish. That's what it's called. So it's not profanity at all, it's just its name."

So he gets back to the monastery and asked one of the other priests, "I caught this son of a bitch and I wonder if you'd clean it for me?"

"Okay. I'll do that," was the reply.

And the cook came along and said, "Wow! That is a beautiful son of a bitch. Let's have him for supper tonight."

And he said, "Okay."

Well, the new bishop was coming for a visit. None of

them had ever met him before. "That son of a bitch would be a good thing to serve to him," said the cook.

So the priests and the bishop were sitting around the table and the cook came regally walking in with this platter of fish and sets it down. The bishop said, "That is the most beautiful fish I ever saw."

And the little priest down there said, "Well, I caught the son of a bitch."

And the other priest said. "Yes, and I cleaned the son of a bitch."

And the cook said, "Well, I cooked the son of a bitch."

And the bishop looks around to everybody and said, "You know, I didn't know whether I was going to like you people or not. But you assholes are all right."

Joy and I have been lucky enough to travel widely, but Ruidoso is still one of our favorite places. We have a house there on top of a mountain with an unobstructed view of twelve thousand foot high Sierra Blanca which is usually covered with snow in winter. Joy likes us to take a trip out there on weekends, and the weekend starts on Wednesday.

THERE IS A UNIVERSAL LAW that is like a giant apothecary's scale—the kind with the cross arm from which hang two bowls on chains. One of the bowls is marked "Rewards" the other is marked "Service." This law guarantees that the world will "match" what we put in the bowl marked "Service" with our "Rewards." If we want more rewards, we must first give more service. It works every time.

Forty-two

Looking Back and Looking Forward

*God, grant me the ability to be
the kind of person my dog thinks I am.*

SOMETIMES PEOPLE ASK ME about my philosophy of investment. We had a friend named Bill Costa—unfortunately he passed away—who was a homebuilder in El Paso. And he loved to fish and hunt, but mostly fish. In a builders' meeting one time, he was asked, "Bill, if you were to suddenly win the lottery, say you won five million dollars in the lottery, what would you do?"

Everybody expected Bill to say, "I would go fishing and stay fishing." He thought it over for a short while and he said, "I guess that I'd just keep building homes as long as the five million lasted."

That's my philosophy as well. My vocation is my avocation. There is nothing I'd rather do than work. Of course, today I don't work nearly as hard as I did when I was building my business. In fact, I don't feel like I do much work at all. I come to work every morning and Elsa has two newspapers spread out and an urn of ice water and soft music playing, and I start reading the newspapers and from time to time someone comes by to discuss something and then at the end of the day I go home and get spoiled by Joy in the same way. Makes for a pretty nice life.

At times I think back with tremendous gratitude that I was given those Earl Nightingale records with the simple message that "We become what we think about." Since then, I have seen that message repeated over and over again by so many individuals in different times. In Proverbs it says, "As a man thinketh in his heart, so is he." In the New Testament, Jesus tells us in many ways that it is our beliefs and thoughts that will bring forth the abundant harvests sought. Aristotle said, "The energy of the mind is the essence of life." Prentice Mulford told us in the late 1800s that, "Thoughts are Things." Ernest Holmes in his fantastic book *The Science of Mind*, first printed in 1926, goes a step further and teaches us how everything we see is a result of manifestations of our mind. From the 1930s we had many people like Norman Vincent Peale and Napoleon Hill tell us that our thoughts make our world. Edgar Cayce, the sleeping prophet, tells us in his spiritual readings that "Mind is the builder, physical is the result." Albert Einstein said, "Physical concepts are free creations of the human mind, and are not, however they may seem, uniquely determined by the external world." Earl Nightingale in the 1960s, Anthony Robbins in the 1990s, Wayne Dyer with his "Power of Intention," and all of the more recent personal development gurus say the same thing in different ways. A simple message, but the end result is that our thoughts create our reality. There must be a universal truth to this because that message has come to us from religion, science, industry and business for thousands of years. So simple, so hidden, and yet it's everywhere around us.

I tried to teach my children the philosophical principles that have proved so helpful to me. I tried to raise them and teach them to go out and do whatever they want to do in life. I told them that if you do it with the right attitude, and you control your mind and use your thoughts correctly, you can be successful at anything.

Me and daughter Monica. Monica decided she wanted to travel extensively in Europe so she worked hard selling large, expensive homes and within a few years she was able to save enough money to live her dream.

I had them all listen to Earl Nightingale every morning when they were growing up. They have the tools they need and I think each has pursued their own level of happiness. Isn't that what we all do?

Personally, I enjoy and appreciate the relationship I have with each one of my children. Each one gives me something through that relationship that I get from no other person. And when we are all together, we have a good time.

I have four sons, two daughters, ten grandkids and four great-grandkids. My sons are Andy Jay Winton, Gregory Scott Winton, Mark Todd Winton and Richard Jeffery Winton. My daughters are Monica Joy Winton and Kristel Andrea Winton. Andy has three children—Jacklyn (Jackie) Winton Keith, Sara Winton-Luscombe and Ryan Robert Winton. Jackie has two children—Mackenzie Marie Keith and Maddox Robert Keith. Sara has Sonora June Luscombe and Ryan has Finnegan Robert Winton. Scott has two children—Mark Hartley Winton and Jon Thomas Winton.

Me with my daughter and my two beautiful granddaughters. From left: Kiana, Kristel, myself and Aleksa. **(Inset)** *Me with daughter Kristel.*

Jeff has three children—Cara Marie Winton, Laura Elizabeth Winton and Jonathan Jeffery Winton. Kristel has two daughters—Kiana Joy Camino and Aleksa Joy Camino.

El Paso has been a great place to live and work. The airline connections are good. The people are great. The Mexican food is delicious. The weather is wonderful. We sit here with more than three hundred days of sunshine a year. No tornadoes, no earthquakes, no forest fires, mudslides or hurricanes. Thank goodness we have the most boring weather in the world.

Shortly after moving to El Paso in 1975, we met a couple who we later became very good friends with. They are Dan and Tommie O'Leary. We have done business with them over the years by buying land and developed lots from them and Tommie has also done lots of appraisals on homes we build. We have taken many trips with them and have a

Me with my sons, 1996. From left: Jeff, Todd, myself, Scott and Andy.

lot of fun traveling with them. About four years ago, we moved into a subdivision they developed and we built our home on a cul-de-sac. They built next to us. Tommie loves to cook and we love to eat so we eat at their home quite frequently. Tommie is an accomplished pianist and we enjoy old fashioned sing-alongs in the evenings. She plays the songs from when we were younger and we sing and argue with Dan on what the correct words are.

Joy and me with our close friends and neighbors, Dan and Tommie O'Leary.

Winton & Associates, which Herschel and I started in 1988 with a two thousand dollar investment, is now worth over twenty-two million dollars. Today we have more than eighteen business entities. We do land development, homebuilding, insulation and pools. We have over sixty-five hardworking people with us. One day I added up that we provide jobs for a thousand people when you count our subcontractors and suppliers. As of 2012 we build in twenty-two different subdivisions in El Paso and Las Cruces. In 2011 we sold 329 homes. Each one of these companies is important to me, as is the overall financial health of the company and the people who work there.

At the end of every Friday, when all the checks have been written, all the subs have been paid, and all the suppliers have been reimbursed, I look over the accounts of each entity, just to be sure that we have enough cash in the bank. Only then can I rest easy.

We have recently embarked on a number of new projects. We recently acquired a position in Franklin Building Materials, and started a new title company, Great Western Abstract and Title, to perform our closings. We expect both to contribute to our bottom line.

For the future of the company, I believe that things will get better and better. I'm sure that the future will present challenges that are both exciting and inspiring at the same time.

Throughout my life, I have always been blessed with good health, but in the middle of 2010, I was diagnosed with a malignant cancer of the colon. After I got the news, I did what I have always done when faced with adversity: I remembered the teachings that have been essential to my business success. I have always tried to accept the situation without complaint and keep my faith in the future while enjoying the present. In fact, my son Todd tells me that I was telling jokes on the gurney after one of my operations. Too bad I can't remember which jokes they were. Fortunately, they were clean. He said, "They were like grade school jokes."

I remembered the teachings of Earl Nightingale and adopted a positive attitude. I decided that I would eventually recover from my illness and get back to doing what I love: working for my business and my family.

I went to MD Anderson, in Houston, for further testing after my initial diagnosis, and I underwent surgery there for my colon cancer in May 2011. I will have to wear a colostomy bag for the rest of my life. I'm very accustomed to it by now, and have found that it is not any problem.

I had excellent care in Houston. Dr. Miguel Rodriguez-Bigas performed the surgery and he is one of the best in the world. He also has a tremendous team headed by Coleen Reeves. Dr. Charles Butler did some required reconstructive surgery, and I am also grateful to my two oncologists Dr. Michael Overman and his PA, Lan P. Vu in Houston, and Dr. Jesus Gomez and Eric, his PA, in El Paso. We also became close to Melanie Mora, my nurse at Texas Oncology, in El Paso, who administered my four-hour chemo treatments.

When I was in the recovery room at MD Anderson, Joy and I became close to Kimberly Williams, my recovery nurse. We were invited to her celebration when she was given the Caregiver of the Month award. That was quite an honor for her considering there are thousands of healthcare providers at MD Anderson, and we were honored to have been invited. I stood up and spoke a few words about what a special, unbelievable person she is. We usually go out to dinner with her and her daughter when we are in Houston.

On the fourth day after surgery, I developed a blood clot in my left lung. I was treated with Heparin, which almost wiped me out, since I am one of the rare individuals who is allergic to that medication.

After thirty days in the hospital, I was able to go back to El Paso. Within two months, I was back at work. They had told me I would have a six to twelve month recovery, but I have some of that bumblebee in me who doesn't know he is not supposed to fly, and I had things I needed to do.

About six months after my original surgery, follow up examinations revealed that the cancer had spread to my liver. I had surgery in March of 2012. Eight weeks after my surgery, Joy and I went on a two-week trip to Europe.

I want to make one thing very clear. I know that my mind is much more important to my well being than my body. I truly believe that every man controls his own destiny. And I know that my destiny will be a thing of wonder. My intention to live to be ninety-five is still very, very strong, and I absolutely refuse to consider or accept any other possibility.

When I was a small child, maybe five years old, I remember overhearing the doctor make a frightening statement when he came thirty miles out to see me when I was sick. At the end of the examination, a substantial period of time, he motioned to my mother and took her over near the door. They didn't leave the room, they were close by and I heard him say to her, "Mrs. Winton, I might as well prepare you: I don't see how

After my 2011 surgery, me with two of the best doctors one could ever expect to have. **Above**—*Dr. Jesus Gomez from El Paso.* **Right**—*Dr. Miguel Rodriguez-Bigas from Houston.*

this child can possibly make it. So don't be shocked." I don't know how much time went by, I guess two or three days before I woke up. I guess I had been in a coma or something and my mother was sitting by the bed, and when I woke I said, "Boy, I am hungry."

She said, "What would you like?"

And I said, "Peanut butter and crackers." And she started handing me peanut butter crackers as fast as I could eat them. I just could not get enough and they tasted so good!

During this period I remember an experience of rising, almost like a whirlwind. And something was rising round and round me but it's almost like I was in a tube of air or something going up up up. I was reminded of this when I was reading *Life after Life* by Dr. Raymond Moody. My experience taught me that I have joined the ranks of the people who say they have no fear or hesitation about dying.

I think heaven and hell are just states of mind and that God gave us free will over our attitude to decide which we choose to live in. Part of the learning experience of life is to learn to master the way we react to our circumstances. We decide if we have a good day or a bad day and a heavenly life is made up of consecutive good days.

In Christian doctrine we are promised eternal life. I believe we are living it now and eternity is nothing but a continuous series of moments. Our bodies may die, but we do not. And when we pass to that next dimension, in this eternity, without our body, we probably get to continue to live in the heaven or hell we again create with our thoughts in the moments of life in that new dimension.

I have never really thought about what I want written on my tombstone. Maybe: "He became what he thought about."

> *You know what they put on the CPA's tombstone? Here lies old Jeff Jacobs, all figured out.*
>
> *And what they put on the golfer's tombstone? Old golfers never die. They just lose their balls.*
>
> *And what they put on the atheist's tombstone? All dressed up and nowhere to go.*
>
> *And on the hypochondriac's tombstone? I told you I was sick.*
>
> *And on the old maid's tombstone. Who says you can't take it with you?*

I have a feeling that my funeral won't be too big a deal, but there might be some people I know who would like to say a few words of how much they appreciated some of the things that God, through me, have been privileged to do for them.

Me working on the book with my son Scott, without whose help this book would not have happened.

I am very hopeful that the reading of this book by my children, grandchildren, great-grandchildren, and great-great-grandchildren, et cetera will be beneficial. I hope that they will determine from reading the book that hard work, dedication and perhaps most importantly, correct thinking will bring them anywhere in life they may wish to go. This philosophy works for the pursuit of any goal. I have practiced this thinking for most of my life and have enjoyed one of the most wonderful, eventful, satisfying lives of anyone that I have personally ever known.

I CAME ACROSS the following meditation attributed to actor Cary Grant, and felt that it has some good suggestions on how to get along in this world:

Now Lord, you've known me for a long time. You know me better than I know myself. You know that each day I am growing older and someday may even be very old, so meanwhile please keep me from the habit of thinking I must say something on every subject and on every occasion.

Release me from trying to straighten out everyone's affairs. Make me thoughtful, but not moody, helpful, but not overbearing. I've a certain amount of knowledge to share; still it would be very nice to have a few friends who, at the end, recognized and forgave the knowledge I lacked.

Keep my tongue free from the recital of endless details. Seal my lips on my aches and pains: they increase daily and the need to speak of them becomes almost a compulsion. I ask for grace enough to listen to the retelling of others' afflictions, and to be helped to endure them with patience.

I would like to have improved memory, but I'll settle for growing humility and an ability to capitulate when my memory clashes with the memory of others. Teach me the glorious lesson that on some occasions I may be mistaken.

Keep me reasonably kind; I've never aspired to be a saint... saints must be rather difficult to live with.... Yet, on the other hand, an embittered old person is a constant burden.

Please give me the ability to see good in unlikely places and talents in unexpected people. And give me the grace to tell them so, dear Lord.

Thank you God.

Notable People in My Life Not Mentioned Earlier

What I found most frustrating about writing a book is that I have had to leave out so many stories about so many of my good friends. Here, I wanted to acknowledge just some of the people who have had a big impact on my life and who I have special feelings for. Thanks for your talents and generosity and so much more.

In Stigler, Oklahoma

Mac McCrory was the bandleader and a former World War II fighter pilot, someone I thought highly of.

Haskel Head, the owner of a drug store in Stigler where I spent some time hanging out, was always very kind and considerate.

In Clovis, New Mexico

Dr. Lynn W. Abshere was a very close friend. We played tennis together, played racquetball together, dined together and had adult beverages together. A very good friend who has since passed away.

Dr. William P. Hale was a very good friend of mine who used to be kind enough to provide a lot of my transportation to and from high school.

Engle Southard was one of my true heroes in high school. A top athlete in football, basketball and other sports, he played center on the state championship basketball team in 1951. Engle passed away in 2008.

Dr. Gene Walker, a dentist, whom I have kept in touch with for all these years and I appreciate him very much.

Mr. Harry Barton, the choral director who was very instrumental in seeing that I and others learned something about vocalizing. Under his directorship, we put on *South Pacific*, *Oklahoma* and other upscale productions.

R. E. Marshall, Superintendent of Schools, had been football coach when my Uncle Don attended Clovis High in the 1930s. He was an outstanding and unusual gentleman from the South.

Roy Gentry, a competitor, but still a good friend in the real estate business.

Dick Worley, the son and ultimate owner of Worley Mills, the Southwest's largest feed mill. Dick was a good friend and he passed away a few years ago.

Dora Russell, Spanish teacher, who inspired me to become very interested in learning to speak Spanish. Since my high school and college days, I consider myself bilingual.

Jim Hayworth, a real estate broker and long-time friend from Albuquerque, was one of the most flamboyant and mercurial people I have ever known.

Darrell Stilwell came to work selling real estate for me. He wound up being my sales manager.

Jimmie Malone was one of my early girlfriends and, perhaps, the first true love I ever had. My relationship with her taught me a lot about dealing with life and with women. (As if I know.)

Kenneth Cook was the Standard Oil distributor who served the pumps that we used to pump our own gas from in our meat packing company. Kenneth was very considerate of me and frequently took me places with him in his airplane, such as a trip to El Paso, for two or three days one time.

From the Army Days

Dr. Joseph Leroy Denner was a wonderful, outstanding man who was my closest buddy during basic training. He had a strong belief in fairness and standing up for the little man, which he exhibited from time to time. Joe was from a wealthy family in Oklahoma who owned a large bread baking company. He subsequently became a psychiatrist and visited with his wife in Clovis en route to moving to Kansas City.

Sergeant James Clark was the personnel sergeant that I worked for all the time in the Army—an outstanding person.

Sergeant Turnbow, the battalion first sergeant, was a tough, crusty, old master sergeant who taught me a lot about life and the Army.

Chief Warrant Officer Phillip M. Hamilton was my immediate boss above Sergeant Clark working in personnel in the Army.

Milburn Moore was a very close associate in high school who sang baritone in our four-man quartet, along with **Dale Jones**, who sang high tenor. I sang second tenor, and **Levi Break** was the bass. Levi was a wonderful man. A lot of these folks have since departed this earth, Levi being one of them.

Jim Whatley, a very close friend in high school, worked with me at Lyman's Flowers. He turned out to be quite a basketball player and spent a career coaching basketball in Kerrville, Texas.

From the Eastern New Mexico University Days

Professor Orville Branscum, a mentor and an outstanding college professor, taught many of the business classes which I took.

Professor Scott Sieger was a great mentor. He recognized after I had returned from the Army that I was a little more mature, perhaps, than some of the other students. He used to invite me over to his house in the afternoon to have a beer. My son Scott was named after him.

Brooks Moore was a partner in Tommy and Brooks' Food Market in Portales. When I first got out of the Army and started taking university courses I worked for them, carrying out groceries, which brought about my meeting with Mr. and Mrs. Turner.

From the Meat Packing Days

Clarence Worley, father of Dick Worley, previously mentioned, was kind enough to take time and have lunch with me occasionally when I was attempting to manage the meat packing company. He gave me several secrets of business management, which I still employ today.

Dr. Ben Russell, the veterinarian who inspected our meat packing plant, became a very close friend and would take me flying in his airplane from time to time.

Leslie Alford, a big, friendly, happy, kill-floor butcher who I worked with at least two days a week. We were quite a team for the amount of work we could get done in a ten or eleven hour day.

Jerry Christmas joined my little meat packing venture as manager and was a very powerful and strong individual. He taught me many important things.

Bub Snell, a competitor in the business, but a friendly and helpful one who I spent as much time with as possible.

Truman and Dixie Hammitt, owners of a supermarket in Portales, who were true and loyal customers of my company and who continued a friendship long after I left the business.

Leonard Horner, a short order cook in a restaurant I called on, taught me the true art of efficiency. This man could handle six or eight orders simultaneously in a timely manner and produce food that was perfectly prepared. I learned a lot from him.

Jim Claybourne, a refrigeration specialist, tried to keep our old, beat up equipment running properly.

Clyde Rail managed the Clovis Cattle Commission Company during the days my father was running the meat packing plant and, thereafter, when I was running it. Mr. Rail subsequently bailed out First Federal Savings & Loan and took over as its chairman, a job he retained until his death.

Ralph Williams owned a physical therapy center. One time when I had hurt my back, I was sent to Ralph for physical therapy. He influenced me to start lifting weights, which I did religiously for many, many years. I went from a 145-pound weakling to a 190-pound not-so-weakling person.

From the Early Real Estate and Homebuilding Days

Lynelle G. Skarda, the chairman and principal owner of Citizens Bank of Clovis. He was instrumental in advising and helping me as a mentor.

Molly Nieves studied with me to take the real estate exam and was in the same testing class in Albuquerque when I got my real estate license.

Dan Buzzard, an attorney in Clovis, who I truly loved. He kept me from getting in trouble many times and I valued his advice.

Jody Johnson was a very popular and well-known person who I somehow sold on the idea of selling real estate for me. She became extremely successful—subsequently was president of the New Mexico Realtors Association and did outstanding things for the industry.

Finis Holloway, a master carpenter, became my right-hand person in homebuilding. He could perform miracles in getting things completed on time.

Lyle Walker, Jim Hart's law partner in Clovis, was in high school with me, and was an outstanding tax attorney.

Dr. Elwin Crume started as my eye doctor but became a good friend, a partner once in a plane and someone I used to have a lot of fun with.

Delbert Miller, the husband of my sister Becky, was a good friend at one time. He became head of the western division for the Santa Fe Railroad.

Bob Murphy, in Albuquerque, was a very close associate of Ben Abruzzo, who owned a shopping center in Clovis and spent many hours visiting with us on his business trips.

Bob Upton, former president of First National Bank of Clovis, became a very close friend.

Dickie Waters and **Joe Wood** had a bricklaying business and were outstandingly successful and well liked.

People from El Paso

Chuy Enriquez was my first concrete man when I came to El Paso. He still pours concrete at eighty years of age and outworks all of his employees.

Tony Lama, the world-famous boot manufacturer, was a very close friend of Lee Trevino. I first met him at Lee's house for dinner one evening.

Joy and me with our good friends Judy and Tony Lama, 1984.

Tony and his wife Judy were very close friends and people that we loved and appreciated for many, many years. Judy has since passed away, but Tony is still a friend.

General James Maloney, a retired major general, spent more than thirty years in the military, and was the commander at Fort Bliss for the last three-and-a-half years. He is a somewhat recent acquaintance, but a person I appreciate greatly.

Ed Ely was the vice president of the old State National Bank. When I came to El Paso, he was my banker and, subsequently, my banker in Midland, Texas. Even to this day, we maintain a very good and close relationship.

Jim Leonard, an Air Force pilot, left the Air Force as a major and came into homebuilding. He helped run the homebuilding company in Santa Teresa and La Paz in the early days.

Bobby Surrat, a friend of Charlie Crowder's, became a close friend. He assisted with the Horizon Country Club name-change to Emerald Springs Country Club and put together a group of golf course homeowners who were interested in buying the club. Bobby is now deceased, but was a wonderful friend.

Dick Knapp was an early homebuilder and very large land developer. I had the opportunity to know and learn a great deal from him.

Wally Clark was the manager of the Horizon Country Club near El Paso when I first met. Wally was a former commander of an aircraft carrier ship, and was an outstanding manager for the country club. Marty and I hired him to come to Clovis and consult with us as we rebuilt our clubhouse.

Randy O'Leary is the organizer and owner of Desert View Homes in El Paso, Las Cruces, New Mexico, and Colorado Springs, Colorado. Randy's company has grown to be the forty-third largest homebuilding company in the United States.

Russell Hansen, a young enthusiastic land developer, has proven to me repeatedly that he is a person of integrity and honesty. I have stories about him which would scarcely be believable.

Mark Ferguson, the president of D. R. Horton's homebuilding operation in New Mexico, has become a very close friend and I value his input and his judgment.

Bob Kotarski and his wife Ann are great friends. The best bank relationship I have ever had started with Bob when he was at State National Bank. When he opened the El Paso branch for City Bank out of Lubbock, we of course followed.

Gary Sapp, the president of Hunt Communities, has become a good friend in the last few years. He is knowledgeable, articulate and a lot of fun to spend time with.

Jaime Zubiate is a young man whose career I have watched since he was bending tin for Richard and Ruben Onsures. I have enjoyed watching him succeed and I have enjoyed his and his wife Anna's friendship and support.

Javier Ruiz, a young man with a vision, sold us on Energy Star and built a business that started with us as his first customer. He is always three steps ahead of the crowd and we appreciate his friendship.

Ann Morgan Lilly, District 1 representative on the El Paso City Council, has worked with us very closely on several important projects. She is one of the most straightforward, honest and dedicated civil servants I have ever known.

Ted Neergaard and **Connie Neergaard** were partners with us in homebuilding in Carlsbad, New Mexico. Ted always has been a very honest and straightforward individual who has always run his business in an outstanding fashion.

Me with Ann and Rut Lily.

Influential Public Figures Whose Philosophies Helped Me

Cavett Robert, a retired attorney, became a very well-known public speaker. We became close friends and we had him visit and give talks for my sales force in Clovis many years ago. The last time I saw him was in El Paso at a Positive People rally along with Dr. Norman Vincent Peale and Zig Ziglar and other well-known speakers.

Ernest Holmes wrote the book *The Science of Mind* which has been extremely instrumental to me. I have recommended it and given copies to many people.

Appendix A.
Poems to Live (and Laugh) By

A Reluctant Investor's Lament

by Don Weill

I hesitate to make a list
Of all the countless deals I've missed;
Bonanzas that were in my grip
I watched them through my fingers slip;
The windfalls which I should have bought
were lost because I over-thought;
I thought of this, I thought of that,
I could have sworn I smelled a rat,
And while I thought things over twice,
Another grabbed them at the price.
It seemed I always hesitate,
Then make my mind up much too late,
A very cautious man am I
And that is why I never buy.
When tracts rose high on
Sixth and Third,

The prices asked I felt absurd;
Whole block-fronts bleak and black with soot—
Were priced at thirty bucks a foot!
I wouldn't even make a bid,
But others did—yes, others did!
When Tucson was cheap desert land,
I could have had a heap of sand;
When Phoenix was the place to buy,
I thought the climate much too dry!
"Invest in Dallas—That's the spot!"
My sixth sense warned me I should not,
A very prudent man am I
And that is why I never buy.
A corner here, ten acres there,
Compounding values year by year,
I chose to think and as I thought,
They bought the deals I should have bought.
The golden chances I had then
Are lost and will not come again,
Today I cannot be enticed
For everything's so overpriced.
The deals of yesteryear are dead;
The market's soft, and so's my head!
Last night I had a fearful dream,
I know I wakened with a scream;
Some Indians approached my bed—
For trinkets on the barrelhead,
(In dollar bills worth twenty-four,
And nothing less and nothing more),
They'd sell Manhattan Isle to me,
The most I'd go was twenty-three.
The redman scowled: "Not on a bet!"
And sold to Peter Minuit.

At times a teardrop drowns my eye
For deals I had, but did not buy;
And now life's saddest words I pen
"If only I'd invested then!"

The Homebuilder's Prayer

Lord, I just bought me a parcel of earth.
I paid a lot more than the damn stuff is worth,
But disdainful of cowardice and not one to yelp,
I've gotten a hunch that this time I'll need help.
Help my engineer, with his bounds and his metes,
Come up with some lots in proportion to streets.
And I will be grateful if you'll bequeath
That the dirt on the top is the same underneath.
Protect me from canvassers carrying petitions,
Resolute councils, and planning commissions.

Find me a house plan I won't have to steal,
With space for the dough, packing buyer appeal.
Provide me a lender who thoughtfully reckons
That skimpy commitments create heavy seconds.
And while we're on money, please have them to set
A few bucks aside for the things I forget.
Grant me swift sales, not by house but by block
So interest on dead ones won't put me in hock.
Protect all my homes from the vandal's low blow,
With up righteousness neighbors, and kids who can't throw.
And then when they're sold and I drive out their way,
Let my buyers yell, "Hi," when I pass, never, "Hey."

The Golden Years

The golden years have come at last.
I cannot see.
I cannot pee.
I still can chew, but cannot screw.
My body's drooping.
I have trouble pooping.
I look like hell.
I'm sure I smell.
The golden years have come at last.
The golden years can kiss my ass.

The Fisherman's Prayer

God, grant that I may live to fish until my dying day.
When I've made my final cast and life has slipped away,
I pray that God's great landing net will catch me in its sweep
And in His mercy God will judge me big enough to keep.

Appendix B.
Books that Have Made Me a Success

I HAVE READ thousands of books, but the ones I have listed below stand out as having had the greatest influence on my life. Read them, enjoy them and most of all learn from them.

How to Win Friends and Influence People by Dale Carnegie
The Power of Positive Thinking by Norman Vincent Peale
Think and Grow Rich by Napoleon Hill
The Magic of Believing by Claude Bristol
Psycho Cybernetics by Dr. Maxwell Maltz
Awaken the Giant Within by Anthony Robbins
The Secret by Rhonda Byrne
The Science of Mind by Ernest Holmes
What to Say When You Talk to Yourself by Shad Helmstetter
The Religions of Man by Huston Smith

Appendix C.
Ten Things to Look for When Buying a New Home

No matter what kind of home you are looking for, here are the ten most important things to consider before making what may be the most important financial decision of your life. Of course, we would like you to buy a home from us, but we realize we do not have something for everyone. There is a good chance we have one for you, though.

1. Location, Location, Location

This is an old adage, but it is really true. Location can be looked at from the perspective of the region, the area, the school district and its attendance boundaries, the location within the neighborhood, and even the place along the spectrum of values in the neighborhood.

2. Orientation

Orientation can make all the difference in the world in how you might use your outdoor space or take advantage of natural breezes, solar gain, etc. For instance, a western-facing back yard will be less desirable if you expect to spend late afternoons outside in the back yard.

3. Design/Function/Landscape

Look at the house and see if it meets your current needs. How does the plan flow? Imagine how it would be living there at different times within a twenty-four hour period. Does the master bedroom have the privacy you want? Are the kids too far away when they might cry out at two in the morning? Is there space for hobbies or favorite pastimes? Does the kitchen work? Would you have to walk too far from the sink to the refrigerator while cooking a meal? These are questions that only you can answer, but you will be happier if you think them out as you decide on a home. Landscaping is also something important to consider because it can enhance or detract from a pleasing appearance. It can also overcome orientation issues.

4. Amenities

Does the house have amenities that will enhance your living there? Do you like the romance of a fireplace? Or would you use a spa to relax at the end of a long day? Are the appliances up to your standard??

5. Energy Efficiency

More and more energy usage will impact your ability to live comfortably in a home and your ability to sell that home. Older homes are not built as tight as new ones. Was the house built for certain heating or cooling systems that have been changed or retro-fitted? For instance, if a house had evaporative cooling and was changed to refrigerated air, was the house properly weather-proofed to help allow more efficient operation of the system? Some experts predict that sellers will one day require an energy audit at the time they sell the home.

6. Quality

You can see quality. What are the cabinets made out of? What about the counter tops? The flooring? Cheap carpet or nice tile? Shower stalls and bath surrounds? How are the wood joints? Do doors stay in the position you leave them or do they swing a direction? There are all sorts of telltale signs of quality in a home.

7. Room for Change

Can you add on a room one day? Do some of the rooms offer flexibility for different uses? Can you age in place? Are the bathroom doors too narrow?

8. Resalability

Will other people want to buy this home if you try to sell it? Can it appeal to a broad range of people, or does it have a limited market? For instance, does a two-story house with the master bedroom upstairs appeal to as many people as a single-level home?

9. Attractiveness

Is the house attractive? Does it have nice curb appeal? Does it match the neighborhood? Is it nice looking inside? Is it dark or light or neutral?

10. Market conditions

Is it a buyer's or a seller's market? Can I get expenses paid by the seller or is the market so hot I may have to bid over the asking price to get the home? Would the house I buy survive sharp swings in values as the market changes? How stable is the market?

Winton & Associates, Inc.

6300 Escondido Drive
El Paso, Texas 79912
915-584-8629
www.wintonhomes.com
www.elpasoaccenthomes.com